TWAYNE'S WORLD AUTHORS SERIES
A Survey of the World's Literature

SPAIN

Janet W. Díaz, University of North Carolina at Chapel Hill
EDITOR

Francisco Ayala

TWAS 450

Francisco Ayala

FRANCISCO AYALA

By ESTELLE IRIZARRY
Georgetown University

TWAYNE PUBLISHERS

A DIVISION OF G. K. HALL & CO., BOSTON

Library of Congress Cataloging in Publication Data

Irizarry, Estelle.
  Francisco Ayala.

  (Twayne's world authors series ; TWAS 450 : Spain)
  Bibliography: p. 157 - 62
  Includes index.
    1. Ayala, Francisco, 1906 -   —Criticism and interpreta-
tion.
PQ6601.Y3Z696   868'.6'209   77-5659
ISBN 0-8057-6287-6

To my mother, Ceil Roses

Contents

About the Author

Estelle Irizarry, Associate Professor of Spanish and Spanish-American literature at Georgetown University, holds a B.A. degree from Montclair State College, M.A. from Rutgers University and Ph.D. from The George Washington University.

Professor Irizarry is the author of *Teoría y creación literaria en Francisco Ayala* (Madrid: Editorial Gredos, 1971), an annotated critical edition of Ayala's *El rapto, Fragancia de jazmines y Diálogo entre el amor y un viejo* (Barcelona: Editorial Labor, 1974), and numerous articles on the same author. She prepared a scholarly edition of the Argentine classic *Martín Fierro* for Clásicos Ebro in 1975 and recently published in Spain *La inventiva surrealista de E. F. Granell* (Madrid: Insula, 1976).

Professor Irizarry has written a monthly section on Hispanic culture in the United States for the Mexican magazine *Nivel* since 1970 and has contributed many studies of Spanish and Spanish-American literature to scholarly journals, such as *Insula, Cuadernos Hispanoamericanos, Cuadernos Americanos, Papeles de Son Armadans, La Torre, Espiral* and *Inti.* She has also written chapters in several volumes of collective criticism published in Spain, Mexico and the United States.

Preface

Francisco Ayala's prominent place in contemporary Spanish letters is a unique success story for a number of reasons. First of all, it is unusual for someone who has not wholly identified himself as a novelist to be taken seriously as such. In Ayala's case, critics invariably marvel at his accomplishments in several disciplines. Books and articles about him—and this one is no exception—are inevitably prefaced by citing his eminence as a sociologist, political scientist, literary critic, Hispanist, professor, essayist, and novelist. Ayala rather jokingly recognizes his disconcerting public image in his apocryphal prologue to *Los usurpadores (The Usurpers)*, and in his introduction to a volume of *Cuentos*, he asks: "Well, what am I?: A novelist? An essayist? A professor? If a professor, of what? Of political and social sciences? Of literature? Because, after all, my writings don't seem to lend themselves in any way to those disparaging comfortable designations by which the garrulous diversity of intellectual products is usually punished."

Ayala's own assessment of his work is that his place in Spanish intellectual history will be determined primarily by his literary inventions. The present volume, therefore, focuses mainly upon his fictions, organizing them chronologically by titles or identifiable tendencies, but includes two chapters, prior to a discussion of his latest narrative production, which treat his sociological and literary essays. Ayala's essays and fictions are so closely interrelated that they complement and elucidate each other. Both areas of creation show concern with examining the moral fiber of a world increasingly divested of values. While the essay provides a means of studying collective social phenomena, the novel allows unlimited scrutiny of the plight of individual characters in what Unamuno called "intrahistory." It takes a master novelist to transmute materials which may lend themselves equally to discursive lucubrations into legitimate works of literary art, and fortunately, Ayala's achievements in this regard are unquestionable.

Another reason for our author's uniqueness is that although he belongs to that "lost generation" of Spanish intellectuals dispersed throughout the world by the Civil War of 1936, he has made a spectacular return to prominence in the country from which he lived in exile for many years. Winning the prestigious *Premio de la Crítica* in 1972 represents a formidable accomplishment since, unlike many other literary prizes, the identity of the author is known when the selection is made by a board of Spain's most distinguished critics. Ayala's return to the Spanish literary scene was probably facilitated by his prudence and discretion in avoiding attacks upon individuals or groups in his literary works. During approximately a decade after the Spanish Civil War, he virtually refrained from writing fiction and when he resumed this activity, he decided to probe the fundamental problems of man's relation to man, rather than to express specific or personal problems which might have aggravated already hostile feelings.

After the "discovery" of Ayala for the Spanish reading public by José R. Marra-López in his *Narrativa española fuera de España (Spanish Narrative Outside of Spain)* in 1963, followed by Keith Ellis's monograph *El arte narrativo de Francisco Ayala* in 1964, his reputation as a writer of fiction became firmly established and his works attracted the attention of European critics as well as those who already knew him in America. Two more monographic books dealing with his work were added to his critical bibliography in 1971 and 1972, but up to the present time, no book has been published in English. Perhaps this is due in part to the desire of the writers to contribute further toward Ayala's reincorporation into Spain's literary scene.

An additional difficulty in solidifying Ayala's image as a writer is that he has a habit of changing his literary expression constantly, which can prove very distressing to critics and investigators. While there are consistent underlying themes in his creations, Ayala uses his craft to experiment with different techniques, structures, and modes of writing, so that a reading of one of his books can at best provide a partial view of his total production, whose essential characteristic is variety. This study, which cannot purport to be exhaustive, attempts to provide a critical evaluation and analysis of all his work. It is designed to point out both constant and variable factors in his work, and to present a coherent vision of Francisco Ayala as a humanist and novelist. This study is the result of several readings of Ayala's complete works and includes a bibliography of hundreds of secondary sources, which, despite their scope, leave many areas of his creation virtually untapped. I have tried to fill these gaps, which occur principally in the criticism of his earlier works, *Historia de macacos (Monkey Story)* and his most recent fictions.

Ayala's success is also remarkable because he has not been influenced by the contemporary literature of the Hispanic world. He is more easily compared to masters of Spanish literature like Rojas, Cervantes, Quevedo, Galdós and Unamuno than to present-day writers. Aloof from literary fads, cliques and movements, he follows the Cervantine concept of the modern novel as each author's own inimitable instrument of scrutinizing the problem of man's destiny, drawing from one's own vital experiences transmuted by the intangible quality commonly called literary genius into works of art.

Ayala's fiction illustrates his theory that literature should be for everyone, offering each reader the opportunity to enjoy it according to his capabilities and sensitivities. Thus, the less intellectual reader may be fascinated by his stories and their humor or horror, while the more erudite can delight in the density, fine irony, ambiguity and veiled allusions to works of art, music, philosophy, and literature, which challenge the most wary reader. It is obvious that we are dealing with an author who is himself a brilliant literary critic and theorist, very conscious of his craft. I suspect that it is difficult for critics to surprise him, for he is one of his own most penetrating self-analysts, although he always stops short of self-evaluation or criticism in essays, prologues and interviews. Readers and critics are faced with the challenging job of discovering all the subtleties and resolving the ambiguities placed there by a very sagacious author who is not beyond playing tricks on his readers. Above all, Ayala is a hermetic author who falsely gives the impression of being transparent or even autobiographical. This makes interpretation of his works a very risky business, but at the same time an exciting task, even though it may evoke polemics and differences of opinion among his critics.

This book hopes to provide readers, scholars and investigators with a general portrait of not only an extraordinary Spanish writer but a first-rate world author. His own criteria, expressed in his books of literary theory, for judging the worth of contemporary works is to compare a novel, not just to others of its time and country, but rather with the finest universal classics of all time. Using this most demanding criteria, it is not at all an exaggeration to compare his own ample body of fiction to that of the most celebrated international novelists in stature and importance.

In conclusion, it should be clarified that all direct quotations cited in the text and titles appearing in English represent my own translations.

Chronology

1947   In Argentina, founds the magazine *Realidad* and publishes his monumental *Tratado de sociología (Treatise on Sociology)*.

1949   *Los usurpadores (The Usurpers)* and *La cabeza del cordero (The Lamb's Head)* published.

1950   Moves to Puerto Rico, where he lives until 1958. Organizes the School of General Studies at the University of Puerto Rico and directs the university press. Publishes *La invención del Quijote (The Invention of the Quijote)*, essays.

1951   Travels to France and Italy, first of many European trips.

1952   Publishes *Introducción a las ciencias sociales (Introduction to the Social Sciences)*.

1953   Founds the journal *La Torre* in Puerto Rico.

1955   Publication of *Historia de macacos (Monkey Story)*, fictions.

1956   *El escritor en la sociedad de masas (The Writer in Mass Society)* and *Breve teoría de la traducción (Brief Theory of Translation)* published in Mexico.

1957   Trip to Near East and India.

1958   Moves to New York. Professor of Spanish literature at Rutgers University. Publishes his celebrated novel *Muertes de perro (Dog's Death)* and *La crisis actual de la enseñanza (The Present Crisis in Education)*.

1959   Head of the Spanish Department at Bryn Mawr College. Publication of *Tecnología y libertad (Technology and Freedom)*.

1960   First trip to Spain since the civil war, and the beginning of yearly trips there. Publication of *Experiencia e invención (Experience and Invention)*, literary essays.

1962   Teaches at New York University and publishes *El fondo del vaso (The Bottom of the Glass)*, sequel to *Dog's Death*.

1963   Publication of *El as de Bastos (The Ace of Clubs)*, fictions, and books of essays: *De este mundo y el otro (About This World and the Other One)*, *Realidad y ensueño (Reality and Dream)*.

1965   Publishes *El rapto (The Abduction)*, short novel, and the book of essays *España, a la fecha (Spain, at Present)*.

1966   Professor of Spanish literature at the University of Chicago.

1969   *Obras narrativas completas (Complete Narrative Works)* published by Aguilar in Mexico.

1970   Publication of *Reflexiones sobre la estructura narrativa, (Reflections on Narrative Structure)*.

Chronology

1971   *El jardín de las delicias (The Garden of Delights)* published.

1972   Compilation of *Los ensayos: Teoría y crítica literarias (Essays: Literary Theory and Criticism)* published by Aguilar. *The Garden of Delights* is awarded the Critics' Prize in Spain.

1973   Teaches at the Graduate Center of the City University of New York.

1977   Visiting professor at the University of Illinois at Chicago Center. Is awarded the degree of doctorate *honoris causa* from Northwestern University.

CHAPTER 1

A Life in Three Worlds

FRANCISCO Ayala's life spans three continents, and he has left his mark in each of them. His story begins, according to a baptismal register, on March 16, 1906 at one a.m. at 11 Canales Street in Granada, where Francisco de Paula was born, the son of Doña María de la Luz García-Duarte González and Don Francisco Ayala Arroyo.[1] This particular source is valuable because it provides positive documentation identifying the obscure prologuist of *The Usurpers*, F. de Paula A. G. Duarte, as none other than the author himself.

Granada, it will be remembered, was the last stronghold of the Moors in Spain, from which they were routed by the "Catholic Kings" Fernando and Isabel in 1492. Francisco Ayala was raised in this picturesque and historical southern city, the oldest of eleven children. Keith Ellis's book on Ayala gives a fairly complete picture of his professional career up to 1963, with some interesting personal glimpses, such as a letter from his brother Eduardo explaining that their father, orphaned from adolescence, was a noble-spirited but unfortunate businessman, while their mother, who had been educated beyond the usual level of those times, valiantly shared the economic ruin which marked their early environment.[2]

Young Francisco originally intended to dedicate himself to art, for his mother had done some painting, and he had also demonstrated a talent in that field like other notable Spanish writers before him, for example, Benito Pérez Galdós and Gustavo Adolfo Bécquer. He was an avid reader as a child and even wrote stories which have been lost.

Ellis reports an incident described by Eduardo which occurred in the kindergarten run by the Order of Saint Vincent of Paul, which young Francisco attended. A "not very clean" satirical poem had been written in a bathroom, and though Francisco was under suspicion, it seemed unbelievable that such verses could have been penned by a child his age, so the author remained anonymous, marking the humble beginnings of a literary career not devoid of satire.

I   The Artist as a Young Man

In 1921, when our author was fifteen, his family moved to Madrid, leaving him behind in Granada to finish school. Two years later, he began studies at the University of Madrid and wrote for several publications in the capital. His acceptance into Madrid literary circles came at the tender age of nineteen, after the publication of his first novel, *Tragicomedia de un hombre sin espíritu (Tragicomedy of a Man Without a Spirit)* in 1925, which was shortly followed by *Historia de un amanecer (Tale of a Dawn)*. During this time, his stories and literary articles were carried in Ortega y Gasset's prestigious *Revista de Occidente* and in *La Gaceta Literaria*. In 1929 he was awarded a degree in law from the University of Madrid and a scholarship to study political science and sociology in Germany for a year. The next year, in Berlin, he married a native of Chile, Etelvina Silva Vargas, affectionately known as Nina. The young author continued to publish his writings, in line with the vanguard modes which were prevalent in Europe during those years, and completed his doctorate in law at the University of Madrid. There he taught as an Assistant Professor of Law and published a booklet in 1932 entitled *El derecho social en la Constitución de la República española (Social Law in the Constitution of the Spanish Republic)*. Successful in surmounting the competition for academic positions known as *oposiciones*, Ayala was named Professor of Political Law in 1934, the same year his daughter Nina was born.

II   Ayala in South America

When the Spanish Civil War broke out in 1936, the young professor was on a lecture tour which took him to Uruguay, Chile, Paraguay and finally Argentina. Ayala's subsequent return to Spain is not mentioned in Ellis's biography. If he had not been in Spain at the time of the war, it would be only natural that his treatment of the conflict should be "oblique," as Ellis calls it, rather than direct. However, since Ayala was indeed present, his oblique treatment is essentially an aesthetic posture. Later he spent eight months in Prague, serving as Secretary of the Republic's legation there, followed by several weeks in France and two months in Cuba. In 1939, our author immigrated to Argentina, where he resided until 1950, with the exception of one year, 1945, spent teaching functionaries in Brazil. While a professor at the Universidad del Litoral and the Colegio Libre de Estudios Superiores in Argentina, he published various essays and in 1947, his three-volume *Tratado de Sociología (Treatise on Sociology)*. He founded the magazine *Realidad: Revista de Ideas* and translated numerous works of European authors into Spanish. He published literary criticism in the now defunct journal *Sur* and in the daily, *La Nación*, where his articles continue to appear today. Ayala made many friends in Argentina—Jorge Luis Borges, Eduardo Mallea, H. A. Murena and other writers.

Our author had not published fiction since his "Erika en el invierno" ("Erika Facing Winter") of 1930, but in 1944 *El Hechizado (The Bewitched)* was published and was immediately heralded as a first-rate piece of fiction by several critics, among them Borges. Five years later, the publication of this work and other narrations in a volume entitled *Los usurpadores (The Usurpers)*, followed the same year by still another book of short fictions, *La cabeza del cordero (The Lamb's Head)*, revealed that Ayala had indeed been writing imaginative works as early as 1939 and that he had already become a different and much more polished novelist.

III   *Ayala in North America*

Argentina under the dictator Juan Perón proved to be a suffocating atmosphere for our writer, so in 1949, when the rector of the University of Puerto Rico, Jaime Benítez, invited Ayala to organize the basic courses of the School of General Studies and to direct the university press, he accepted. Benítez was a far-sighted educator who recognized the importance of the Spanish intellectuals in exile and tried to attract them to his institution. In 1951, Ayala traveled to France and Italy, the first of many subsequent trips to Europe. At the University of Puerto Rico he founded in 1953 the magazine *La Torre*, still one of the major humanistic journals published in the Spanish language. Ayala and his family continue to maintain a close friendship with Jaime Benítez, who was congressman from Puerto Rico from 1973 to 1977, and his family.

During his years at the University of Puerto Rico, Ayala was a widely solicited speaker in Latin American and United States universities and published *Historia de Macacos (Monkey Story), El escritor en la sociedad de masas (The Writer in Mass Society)* and *Breve teoría de la traducción (Brief Theory of Translation)*. He traveled to the Near East and India in 1957.

In 1958, the same year in which his celebrated novel *Muertes de perro (Dog's Death)* was published, our author came to Rutgers University in New Brunswick, New Jersey, where he continued to teach one evening a week after accepting the position of head of the Spanish Department at Bryn Mawr College the following year. During this time, when I was studying for my master's degree at Rutgers, I first became acquainted with Ayala. We had no idea that our professor was a novelist, and when someone discovered one of his books of essays, *Tecnología y libertad (Technology and Freedom)*, we passed it from one to another with great interest.

A humanist who refused to be restricted by academic "specialization," Ayala's interests spanned the literature of the Spanish Golden Age and the twentieth century, Galdós, and the "Generation of Ninety-Eight." His most memorable traits as a professor were his respect for students and his interest and patience in hearing our ideas. His determination to elicit our responses to the readings was of vital importance to him. His lectures gave the impression of being delightfully informative, spontaneous chats, but they were filled with profound concepts. Never pedantic or overbearing, Ayala enjoyed telling anecdotes about authors and books, making apparent his ability as a superb story teller. He would go to great lengths to help us think for ourselves and it was nothing for him to spend a few hours with a student in the library, helping to translate an article from Italian or German for a term paper. He taught us to read, investigate and think, not to classify and memorize. Ayala is extremely sociable and gregarious, and this was particularly noticeable in our pre-class *tertulias* (gatherings) at the student center, where almost all his graduate students used to come at least a half-hour early before each class session of some two and a half hours, just to converse with our professor about the most diverse themes over a cup of coffee.

In 1960 Ayala visted Spain for the first time since the Civil War. Since then he spends part of each year there. In 1962 he accepted a position at New York University, but came to Rutgers for Saturday graduate classes. His novel *El fondo del vaso (The Bottom of the Glass)* was published in that same year, followed shortly by *El as de Bastos (The Ace of Clubs), El rapto (The Abduction)* and several books of essays. It was during this period, in 1963, that José Marra-López brought Ayala's name to the fore in Spain, where he was virtually unknown, by dedicating a chapter in his book *Narrativa española fuera de España (Spanish Narrative Outside of Spain)* to him. The next year Keith Ellis's book, previously mentioned, contributed further to fostering a reunion between our author and the Spanish reading public, which culminated in 1970. On June 3 of that year, a group of Spanish intellectuals published a formal welcome to Francisco Ayala in their newspapers, praising the rediscovery of this great novelist by his native land as an event to be brought to public attention. It was signed by such notable authors as Vicente Aleixandre, Dámaso Alonso, Antonio Buero Vallejo, José Luis Cano, Camilo José Cela, Miguel Delibes, Paulino Garagorri, Carmen Laforet, Pedro Laín Entralgo, Rafael Lapesa, Francisco Ynduráin and Alonso Zamora Vicente.

By 1966 Ayala, who had attracted considerable attention in the Hispanic world, was invited by the University of Chicago to teach two trimesters, an arrangement which made it possible for him to travel to Spain for more extended periods of time. The birth of his granddaughter Juliet Mallory created yet another interest for an already diversified humanist.

In 1969, the prestigious Aguilar Publishing Company issued Ayala's *Obras narrativas completas (Complete Narrative Works)* and three years later, his literary writings in *Los ensayos: Teoría y crítica literaria (Essays: Literary Theory and Criticism)*. The same year his *El Jardín de las delicias* (The Garden of Delights) was awarded the Critics' Prize. In 1973 he accepted the offer of the City University of New York to teach at its Graduate Center. This enabled him to be near his family and the home he had always maintained in Manhattan since 1958.

In April 1976, in honor of Ayala's seventieth birthday, the Spanish Book Center in New York hosted a magnificent reception organized by Rosario Hiriart, author of two books on the novelist. The bookstore was crowded with well-wishers from far and near, among them a number of his critics, including Rodrigo Molina, Ildefonso-Manuel Gil, Adrián García Montoro, Nelson Orringer, Mary Ellen Bieder, and myself, and, of course, his wife and daughter. Never was it more evident that chronological years are a deficient measure of human age. In view of Ayala's enviable vitality and creativity, one could say that he became seventy years young in 1976.

As for his writing, our author noted in an interview with Andrés Amorós, published in *Confrontaciones (Confrontations)*, that he writes unhurriedly. "I have too much respect for literary fiction to submit myself to the conditions of professionalism," he stated, revealing further that although he can write an article about literature or sociology with ease and rapidity, when he composes fiction, he spends hours editing just one paragraph.[3] Ayala works in his New York apartment, surrounded by books and paintings, and on his enormous desk a portable typewriter is always uncovered and ready for action. He also does part of his writing at the beach in Spain and at his Madrid apartment which Andrés Amorós describes as very large, with modern furniture that contrasts pleasantly, in obvious symbolism, with some decorative details of popular Spanish craftsmanship.[4] The apartment is in an older building which is centrally located in the capital, near the Plaza of Cibeles.

Fame hasn't changed Ayala; he is still the same as when I met him eighteen years ago: a warm person with a quick and penetrating sense of humor, who enjoys literature, theater, art and conversation. As for details of our author's personal life, they cannot reliably be gleaned from his works, filled with premeditated traps for the unsuspecting reader in search of autobiographical revelations, nor is it likely that they are forthcoming from his own pen, since he is prone to use his narrative ingenuity to protect his privacy. Ayala is, on the other hand, not at all reluctant to discuss his views, preoccupations and attitudes in conversations and interviews, but, for that matter, these are largely discernible in his works.[5]

CHAPTER 2

Early Novels

F RANCISCO Ayala initiated his career in literature at the age of eighteen with a surprisingly mature novel bearing the suggestive title *Tragicomedia de un hombre sin espíritu (Tragicomedy of a Man Without a Spirit)*. According to his own testimony in the prologue of *La cabeza del cordero (The Lamb's Head)*, written twenty-four years later, his first novel was greeted favorably by the critics. It was followed the next year by a shorter novel, *Historia de un amanecer (Tale of a Dawn)*, which was received with the "all too normal commentary of the critics" and left the author feeling dissatisfied and uncertain of the future direction he should take. No doubt influenced by Ayala's own unenthusiastic comments, few critics have re-examined these first novels which, while they might not be Ayala's masterworks, reveal the emergence of a fine writer and thinker. This is the period of his literary career which has been least treated and understood, but which is basic for understanding his later creations.

I Tragicomedia de un hombre sin espíritu
(Tragicomedy of A Man Without a Spirit)

This novel begins as the narrator receives a note from a casual friend, Miguel Castillejo, who announces his imminent departure and asks him to take charge of his effects. Among these, the narrator finds a manuscript in which Miguel describes his youth as a solitary hunchbacked child, comforted only by his books and by an understanding father who was later imprisoned for revolutionary activities. From this point, the narration continues in the third person, as Miguel manages a modest existence and resigns himself to a loneliness partially alleviated by a few friendships and books. Lured to a tryst by a seemingly sincere love letter, he finds himself the victim of a cruel practical joke perpetrated by Mariana, the bored

young wife of Don Cornelio, a usurer who thinks that he is Don
Quijote incarnate. His pride deeply wounded, Miguel becomes
deranged to the point of imagining that the spirit of cynicism and
indifference which he had so carefully cultivated as a response to his
physical deformity has been stolen from him by the deceitful
woman and now flies about him in the form of a butterfly. Bent on
vengeance, he plans to murder the young woman in her house.
From his hiding place there, he observes a scene which changes his
mind: Don Cornelio is complacent as Mariana—his "Dul-
cinea"—and his faithful squire Sancho Martínez meet in her room.
Distracted from his vindictive plan by the ridiculousness of the
situation, Miguel realizes that it his healthier to laugh than to
despair. He recovers his reason, but is afflicted with great sadness.
His carpenter friend advises him to leave Madrid and to seek peace
in the country. At the end of the novel, we see Miguel on the train,
contemplating the stars.

As the reader familiar with classical Spanish literature will readily
note, Ayala places his plot firmly within a framework of well-known
literary allusions, a procedure he develops with increased sophistica-
tion in subsequent fictions. Many of the allusions are explicit, such
as Don Cornelio's identification with Don Quijote, and the actual
quotes from Calderón, Bécquer, Espronceda, Larra, Galdós and
Unamuno. Professor Rosario Hiriart comments upon these allusions
as well as others from universal literature (Shakespeare, Ibsen,
Schopenhauer, Hugo and Pope) which fill the novel.[1] It is obvious
that Ayala brought to his ambitious first work many ideas gleaned
from "voracious and diverse readings"[2] and that it represents the
creative assimilation of these literary experiences. What has not
been fully appreciated, however, is the extent to which literary
antecedents are incorporated into the actual texture of the novel.
The implicit and unidentified allusion in the *Tragicomedy* is a type
of experiment whose theoretical importance can only be appreciated upon reading his later essays in *Experiencia e invención
(Experience and Invention)*, which treat the theme of tradition and
originality.

A number of scenes in the novel may be traced to famous literary
works in Spanish, such as Miguel's dream in which he moves aside
to let a funeral procession pass and then sees his own image in the
dead man. The first part recalls an experience recounted in the third
book of the anonymous picaresque novel *Lazarillo de Tormes*
(1554), and the second, which Ayala identifies, is inspired by

Espronceda's *El estudiante de Salamanca* (*The Student of Salamanca*, 1840). The blue butterflies which torment Miguel bring to mind Ruben Darío's famous story *El pájaro azul* (*The Bluebird*) in which a mad poet, in love with an attractive neighbor, feels a bluebird imprisoned within his head. He attempts to release the bird by killing himself following the untimely death of the girl.

The most important literary influence throughout the novel is Cervantes with regard to themes, characters, scenes and stylistic devices. Like many young painters who imitate the great masters in order to perfect their techniques, Ayala tries to emulate Spain's finest novelist, paying homage to his model by means of explicit references. The first discernible Cervantine device is the finding of the manuscript of Miguel Castillejo, like that of the Moorish writer Cide Hamete Benengeli which Cervantes purports to have discovered. The "tragicomedy" of the title, while an obvious allusion to *La tragicomedia de Calisto y Melibea* (*The Tragicomedy of Calisto and Melibea*), Fernando de Rojas's fifteenth-century work, also reflects the two sides of Quijotesque behavior, which in a later study of the novel in Unamuno, Ayala defines as a combination of the transcendental and the commonplace.[3] There are, in fact, two Quijotesque figures in this novel. One is Don Cornelio, an anachronistic, ridiculous vaudeville character, whose name itself suggests the Spanish word for cuckold (*cornudo*). Like Don Quijote, Don Cornelio thinks that arms make the man and that a sword and a mount are enough to turn him into his hero, but he is a poor comic version, superficial and ineffectual. Miguel Castillejo, on the other hand, is a more authentic Don Quijote. His first name is that of Miguel de Cervantes, and the depreciatory, diminutive suffix added to his place of origin, Castilla, is akin to both the transformation of Alonso Quijano to Don Quij*ote* (augmentative, but also pejorative), and to the traditional designation of knights (Amadís of Gaul and Palmerín of England, after their birthplace). Miguel Castillejo's affinities with Don Quijote are rooted in experiences, not in mere appearances. An examination of his library, like that of Don Quijote's, reveals that he owes his formation to his readings. Like Don Quijote, Miguel finds his goodness thwarted by others' cruelty and recovers his reason after having been the object of a practical joke and having provided a spectacle for an idle aristocracy. His words have a Cervantine flair: "He made great protestations that he was no longer mad, acknowledging that he had been, and amazed at the nature of that madness" (254).

The episode in which Miguel expects to find the young woman he had followed to Don Cornelio's house, but trips instead in the dark onto the bed of a lecherous old lady, reminiscent of the Celestina of Fernando de Rojas's *Tragicomedy*, is also of Cervantine inspiration. It recalls the comedy of errors when Don Quijote mistakes Maritornes for an enamored lady, and when Doña Rodríguez visits his bedroom. Furthermore, the end of Ayala's novel is similar to that of the *Quijote* as Miguel seeks a remedy for his sadness in a rustic setting far from the city, enacting, as it were, Sancho's proposal to the disillusioned Don Quijote that they both dress as shepherds and take to the country. It is no wonder, then, that Miguel Castillejo reluctantly "felt like the hero of a novel" (241).

In addition to the already noted literary influences, Ayala inherited much of the critical spirit of the "Generation of Ninety-Eight." Like Unamuno and Baroja, for example, Ayala criticizes the decadence of Spain, the deplorable condition of the National Library, the poor schools, and the negative aspects of the city of Madrid where *Equality* may be bought for only ten cents because it is a newspaper. Ayala shows a particularly Galdosian pity for suffering children, such as two adolescent girls victimized by the perverse Tagarote, and for those who suffer the pains of poverty.

Diverse views of life are expressed by Ayala's characters. Miguel's pessimism, lack of purpose and emptiness are contrasted to the optimism of a friend, Alberto Durán, who sees and appreciates life's endless variations. Miguel's neighbor, the philosopher Don Ismael, is unsure whether it is more desirable to choose fame, solitude or riches as a way of achieving true independence. The novel has been criticized for imitating nineteenth-century realistic techniques in excessive descriptions of characters, and also for the abrupt transition from first person narrative in the opening chapter to that of third person, resulting in the disappearance of the author-narrator who was originally involved in the plot itself. Despite these reservations, *Tragicomedy of a Man Without a Spirit* is a strong novel principally for its handling of literary material in a creative fashion. It is also valuable in revealing the origin of major themes which reappear in Ayala's subsequent works, such as the role of the writer, the importance of books as a vital experience, the practical joke, and adultery. Here we find one of the constants of Ayala's literary invention: animal imagery associated with human conduct, in symbolic references to the dog, the monkey and the pig, reflecting servility, ridiculousness and greed respectively.

II   Historia de un amanecer (Tale of a Dawn)

In 1926 Ayala published his second novel, *Tale of a Dawn*, which represents a radical departure from the literary climate of *Tragicomedy of a Man Without a Spirit*. It is, in fact, an indication of the future flexibility of the author in adopting varied modes of expression and changing his image as a writer. The novel seems to be included in discussions of his fiction only because it happens to be one of his early works and not because of any intrinsic value. Díez Canedo considered it too abstract and general; Keith Ellis finds it ingenuous and lacking in dramatic intensity; Andrés Amorós concedes only its documentary value.[4] Ayala's reluctance to discuss it and the silence of other critics have been enough to deter its re-examination, but, in spite of certain defects in the handling of retrospective narrative and a contrived romantic interest in providing mates for some of the male leads, it has a good number of things to recommend it. The smooth-flowing third person narrative holds our interest, and the roles assigned to some of the women are not so colorless as critics have suggested.

The novel opens one dawn in which a man who had tried to assassinate "the Prince" is to be hanged before a multitude in the plaza of "the city." The throng anxiously awaits the execution. A group of conspirators has formed an Academy which serves as a forum for their utopian ideas. Don Nazario, an elderly antique dealer, serves as mentor for the group. The most inspirational young leader is Abelardo, who stresses culture rather than violence as a means of refining the political sensibility of the people to lead them to a new social order. Abelardo, however, is not all ideals, for he illustrates his own statement that: "For all we scorn mundane things, how can one do without them?" (329). So complete is his dedication to the cause of the Academy that he lets his friend Darío court the girl he (Abelardo) is attracted to most and contents himself with the favors of his maid. The rest of the Academy includes some effeminate poets, a number of moderates, those with religious qualms, and the somewhat mystical Gabriel León.

Crisanto, son of a friend of Don Nazario, returns from Algiers, where he has become familiar with the ways of violence. He sees his mission as implementing the theories of the Academy, something Abelardo considers "impure." Crisanto gains support and organizes a small army. Estrella, the daughter of Don Nazario, helps convince him of the necessity of sacrificing Abelardo, whose opposition endangers their cause. Crisanto forces the Academy to reach a decision and Abelardo, observing sadly the resulting free-for-all, realizes his defeat and willingly drinks the poison offered him so that the group may be united and his sacrifice may stand as a lasting protest against violence. The novel ends at dawn, with the anonymous voices of an enthusiastic throng ready to attack an ironically "indefinite" enemy, while one voice speaks out against Crisanto.

As we have indicated, there are some interesting female characters in *Tale of a Dawn*. Estrella is responsible for convincing Crisanto that Abelardo must be sacrificed and she incites the doubting leader to positive action. One of the most striking and mysterious creations of the novel is Aurelia, the governor's wife, strangely attracted to the mystical Gabriel León, who preaches austerity, penitence and interior religion, but who is fascinated by the erotic-mystical dedication of the woman to him. Aurelia, in an exalted state, convinces Gabriel to elevate her over the roof, insisting that she feels she can fly. He releases his hold, letting her fall to her death, thereby giving vent to his mixed feelings of love and hate.

Keith Ellis has stated that the irony which characterizes the later works of Ayala is completely lacking in *Tale of a Dawn*, but actually there is a great deal of irony related to social and political themes.[5] The treatment of crowds, for example, emphasizes the ironic truth that today's heroes are often tomorrow's victims. Abelardo wonders whether the masses themselves will become the new oppressors when the tyrants are overthrown. The very first scene of the novel shows the eagerness of a crowd to witness violence, and the last scene presents its participation in violent action. Symbolically trampled by the crowd at the beginning of the novel, Don Nazario exclaims: "Oh people, blind people! What incompetent God guides your steps?" (273).

As if to answer this question, the three main protagonists have Biblical names: Don Nazario (which suggests Nazarene), Crisanto (*Cristo-santo* or Christ-saint) and *Abel*ardo, also called "the master" and "the redeemer," who, like his namesake, is the victim of violence. Ironically, Abelardo is opposed to revolutionary action but is capable of violence against self, implicit in the suicidal act. These are the heroes, temporary gods who will in time be eliminated. The most tremendous irony may be found at the end when an anonymous voice in the crowd comments: "It will be necessary to take the command from this adventurer so that he doesn't abuse his power. After all, who is this Crisanto?" (367). The implications are indeed ironic: There will always be conspirators and it is impossible to please all. Revolutionaries become tyrants. The deposers will in turn be deposed; and here we have one of Ayala's most prominent themes, developed more fully in the stories of *Los usurpadores (The Usurpers)* and in his novel *Muertes de perro (Dog's Death)*.

The title *Tale of a Dawn* underscores this irony, since there are actually three dawns in the novel: the hanging in the first chapter, the morning following the first meeting of the Academy when the cock crows as a symbol of betrayal, and the dawn of active revolution at the end. The first and last each claim a victim in the presence of anonymous masses, and a question seems to be posed: How many new dawns will witness the fall of other leaders?

Keith Ellis considers the lack of concrete representation of the enemy forces as a weakness of the novel; however, by directing his attention to the conspirators and depicting power as a faceless abstraction, Ayala could examine more effectively the phenomena which most interested him: the nature of political power and the responsibility of those who live under tyranny. As is often the case in such governments, the shadow of the Machiavellian despot ("the Prince") falls over the whole city, but the actual presence of the head of state is reserved for only a few. Sinister forces, as we see in the novel, are most readily perceived in such acts as public executions and the harassment of conspirators. In 1958 Ayala directs his attention to an enemy of freedom, the dictator Bocanegra, the embodiment of evil forces in *Dog's Death*, but certainly *Tale of a Dawn* may be considered a preliminary sketch of similar themes in which irony has not yet reached the point of satire as in the later novel.

CHAPTER 3

Vanguard Adventure

THE World War I period in Europe produced various movements of reaction toward traditional concepts of art and literature which may be grouped under the heading of vanguard. Often crossing the boundaries between literature and the plastic arts, the vanguard art of that period included such movements as Dadaism, Cubism, Surrealism and Ultraism which, for the Spanish philosopher José Ortega y Gasset, could be best described as "the dehumanizing of art." The innovations of the vanguard movements are treated in Gómez de la Serna's book *Ismos (Isms)* and in Guillermo de Torre's *Literaturas europeas de vanguardia (European Vanguard Literature)*. José Carlos Mainer, in his introduction to an edition of Ayala's *Cazador en el alba y otras imaginaciones (Hunter at Dawn and Other Imaginative Pieces)*, indicates four characteristics of the Spanish vanguard narrative, notably, the influence of the psychology of Freud and Jung, the increased use of metaphor instead of realistic description, cosmopolitanism, and humor.[1]

Ayala recalls his contact with vanguard literature and his own participation in the movement in his prologue to *The Lamb's Head* where he speaks of the desire of the young writers to break with the past. It was a literature of gratuitous foolishness taken seriously by others and of irresponsible play with words and metaphors, based on "any insignificant thing seen or dreamed, from which pure fiction emerged in the form of a new and affected rhetoric, filled with sensorial images."[2] For Ayala, the vanguard adventure was a lighthearted exercise of verbal agility and wit to which the gravity of the Spanish Civil War and then the Second World War put an end.

In 1929 his book *El boxeador y un ángel (The Boxer and an Angel)* was published, consisting of five pieces of vanguard fiction beginning with the title story, and in the following year, *Cazador en*

30

el alba (Hunter at Dawn), including the story "Erika ante el invierno" ("Erika Facing Winter"), appeared in book form, although the stories had previously been published in Ortega's *Revista de Occidente*. The critics heralded Ayala as a fine writer, for he demonstrated mastery and originality in achieving metaphoric surprise and unusual imagery, both very important ingredients in the vanguard mode.

I *"El boxeador y un ángel" ("The Boxer and an Angel")*

The anecdotal content of this piece is subordinated to a display of metaphorical brilliance with special reference to the world of mechanization and to the newly developed cinema. There is a deliberate attempt to dehumanize man (a breathing chest is compared to an inflated tire) whereas the inanimate becomes humanized ("uncombed, wounded trains"). Some metaphors are presented in chains in a sort of Surrealistic free association, with one image suggesting another and yet another (a smile is described as smoke from a factory; the factory stabs the sky which "bleeds within" and becomes anemic).

The story itself combines the most prosaic with the fantastic. A boxer, accompanied by an angel, tries to find out if he will win his next match. Assured of triumph, he fights his black opponent and, aided by his winged friend when he is about to lose, rises to his feet and to victory. The anecdote provides a sharp contrast between the commonplace reality of the titular boxer and a heroic, mythical world which is being destroyed. The "oracle" which the "hero" consults is a penny arcade metal bird which for a "stipend" takes into its beak a paper which tells his "destiny." While words suggesting epics and myths are converted into ironic images, the word "angel," long a literary hyperbole, becomes a live angel. The boxer's future like that of an epic hero, is hinted at in an omen when the afternoon "couldn't raise itself, victim of the black opponent" (371), but the help of the angel makes it possible to win. Images of shipwreck, anchored ship, hurricane and tempest (of applause) stress the epic struggle of Man against Destiny in the person of an ordinary boxer with a helpful angel. The destruction of myth is enhanced by the use of everyday sports terms such as "manager, ring, stock," given in English, and by the phonetic transcription of primitive sounds: aup, plac, hop, hip.

II "Hora muerta" ("Dead Hour")

Praised by the critics for its extensive and original imagery, "Dead Hour" involves the reader's senses as it presents a vertiginous view of a city as a "gyrating platform," offering quick glimpses of its components: "Station. Roadway, Factory. Aerodrome. University. Circus. Gymnasium. Movie theater." There is a panting rhythm as the use of impressionistic techniques interfere with logical narrative, presenting the people of the city: "Motorist. Chinaman. Navy captain. Boxer. Negro [reminding us of the previous story]."Imagery seems designed to produce metaphorical shock by joining the unexpected, as in the rural-mechanical description of a "mechanic exhausting the udder of his automobile" (377).

With the ease of a camera, the story focuses on a little girl, dressed in white and jumping rope in a schoolyard. Another section of the story takes us to a movie theater where the most diverse themes are juxtaposed: Charlemagne, Hamlet, Chaplin. The film goes into reverse and there are some rather enigmatic impressions of a sad smile, paleness, a fan peeking out and a white, beckoning glove ("dove toward the wind"). The narrator returns to his house, anguished and disoriented. In the next section, the narrator enters an enchanted house of the nineteenth century which he calls a "Cave of Montesinos", recalling the site of Don Quijote's fantastic visions. There he converses with a mask of Beethoven, a white dove, and a window which speaks, while a book opens itself and a tubercular clock coughs. Grabbing a stuffed dog, he runs from the mysterious house and escapes, in the final section, to the schoolyard where little Anita is still jumping rope.

The story is most impressive for its unusual metaphors, panting pace, and cinematic changes of scene. José Carlos Mainer notes the lack of visible plot; however, although it is indeed concealed behind an ingenious display of words, there is a plot which bears some relationship to that of Tragicomedy of a Man Without a Spirit: the crisis of adolescence. In "Dead Hour" this crisis is not explicitly narrated, but must be perceived intuitively in the reappearance of certain symbols of the erotic awakening of the young narrator and his feelings of guilt. Paleness, a white glove, and a fan first appear after the movie, again when the narrator attributes his anguish to the memory of the dying hour that had produced the vision, and finally when he fears their reappearance in the strange house. These are the sensations of a confused adolescent torn between two worlds: that of the innocent Anita in the schoolyard and that of a beckoning woman. His first view of the smile, fan, and glove drives him to seek refuge at home, but there he feels a perverse compulsion to lift the skirts of his bed and then to try to grasp a fish (an erotic symbol) in a bowl. He desperately flings his bottle of Leyden at the piano which emits "adult notes with their adolescent counterparts," stressing the crisis which the narrator experiences.

The enchanted "Cave of Montesinos" to which he has ventured is obviously the house of the tryst, but he becomes frightened before the impending meeting and runs away carrying a stuffed dog ("man's friend," but also a child's consolation). He seeks refuge in the "green garden," symbolically fenced with "green lances," where he joins little Anita in her innocent diversion. The "tac tac" of a clock suggests time going inexorably forward, while the film projected in reverse reflects the innermost aspiration of the narrator, attracted and frightened by the demands of adulthood. Returning to the "trembling water" of Anita's innocence, he finds that even she has the potential of becoming part of the adult world from which he has fled, for embroidered in her white pocket is a "red, red heart" and the King of Spades (in the Spanish card deck, *el Rey de Espadas* or swords—another erotic symbol) which the narrator has given her. The green Garden of Eden will yield to time, and the seven little paper birds the narrator blew away in the enchanted house may well allude to the seven mortal sins.

The theme of the contrasting worlds of childhood and adulthood may be found in later works of Ayala, in various selections of his book *El jardín de las delicias (The Garden of Delights)* and in a vignette entitled "El leoncito de barro negro" ("The Little Black Clay Lion").

III   *"Polar, estrella" ("Polar, Star")*

The unnamed protagonist of this story, "in love, like everyone else, with a movie star," is driven by unrequited love to commit suicide. Together with the vanguard preference for triviality of content and verbal invention, we find here a fascination for the endless possibilities offered by the cinema, then in its infancy. The protagonist's world is distorted by diverse movie phenomena such as the confusing sudden transitions of the newsreel, bicolored reality in which everything assumes shades of black and white, a projection accident which splits Polar's body placing the upper half below the legs, the running of the film in reverse which suggests the possibility of the protagonist's doing the same with memory to forget Polar, and slow motion, the sensation he feels as he floats to his death, for "the god of cinema had disposed his fall *au ralenti* [in slow motion]" (394).

Typically vanguard is the tendency to destroy myth by means of irony. The polar star is another name for the north star which sailors, attracted by its brilliance in the night, follow just as the protagonist follows his Polar in the movies. She is literally a north star since she is Scandinavian (probably a representation of Greta Garbo), and the light of love, depicted as electric voltage, leads the hopelessly enamored fan to his end.

IV   *"Cazador en el alba" ("Hunter at Dawn")*

If critics found retrospective narrative awkwardly handled in "Tale of a Dawn," it is so expertly manipulated in "Hunter at Dawn" that it has not even been noticed. The story itself involves a country youth, Antonio Arenas, who is recruited into the military service, goes to the city where he faces temptations, and is finally saved by his love for Aurora. We first see Arenas as a soldier in the hospital where "pure realities are only visible at 40° (centigrade)," referring to his high fever (the equivalent of 104°). Impressions are seen like incomplete fragments of film as the "fallen hunter" (evidently thrown from his horse), gazing at the white ceiling at dawn, sinks into a state in which his thoughts erupt "unbridled," and in which it is unclear to what extent they recreate his past or are fragments of dream images. His experiences include meeting an "artificial woman," obviously a prostitute, trying to become a boxer, a romantic scene with Aurora, and finally falling asleep in her lap. At the end, however, he awakens first to feel "in the temples the cold fingers of that hour in which hunters station themselves in position at dawn" (437), and then to experience the sensation of chill that he had felt at 4:30 a.m. These sensations recall the hard fingers that he felt oppressing his head in the hospital in the first scene of the story, so we cannot be sure whether he awakens from sleep in Aurora's lap or from feverish delirium in the hospital. In view of the fact that Aurora is the Spanish word for dawn, the confusion is intensified if we remember the classical Homeric image of "rosy-fingered dawn" in the *Iliad*.

This is probably the most surrealistic of Ayala's stories, with the theme of *l'amour-fou* ("mad love"), free association of images, juxtaposition of disparate objects, lack of distinction between dream and memory, and the somewhat absurd confusions among characters which seem to resemble each other (Aurora, her brother, and Arenas's horse, all of them broadnecked). The deliberate destruction of myth is evidenced in hyperbolic comparisons. The hunter Antonio Arenas is a Hercules, Aurora is a marine deity, and the dance hall where the hero meets his love, who stands out among the minor Graces, is appropriately called "The Diana" in honor of the goddess of hunters. This name also evokes connotations of the Spanish word *diana* as the military reveille played at dawn and as the target at which hunters aim, and thereby, is a complex source of images.

The story abounds in uncommon metaphors which cover a wide range of references. The dance hall assumes an unexpected rustic quality for the idyllic romance of the hunter and his prize: "The dance hall was a meadow. A beautiful lyrical meadow where the pianola—cow provident in harmonies—patiently ruminated a roll of juicy green notes" (420). As Professor Ildefonso-Manuel Gil observes, Ayala's metaphors in "Hunter at Dawn" are more intellectual than lyrical because they are contrived in the absence of sentiment.[3] The author uses technical terms *("dermatovértebras"* or dermatovertebrae), word play ("surgent, insurgent"), mathematical terms (the feelings of love between Arenas and Aurora are described as "parallel" and "growing in geometric progression"), aeronautical terms ("chest, impatient aerostat," an airborne love with "the grace of a propeller"), and references to the cinema ("the present consisted of two cinematographic planes").

V *"Erika ante el invierno"* ("Erika Facing Winter")

The plot of this story concerns Erika and her search for her childhood friend Hermann, whom she has not seen since he appeared before her, all grown up, with derby and motorcycle. She too realizes that she is no longer a child. Her uneventful existence is suddenly brightened by a chance meeting on the bus with another boy named Hermann, whose smile and candor cause her to confuse him with her old friend. At the dance hall where they are later supposed to meet, Erika sees a young man who resembles Hermann, but she is confused by his expression of complete indifference. After dancing with a curly-headed Jewish boy, she finds that the uncertain Hermann she had been observing has disappeared. The story is

interrupted by an impressionistic interlude in which it appears that
an eight-year-old boy named Friaul is killed by the knife of his own
father, a butcher. Erika reads a fragment torn from a newspaper
report of the crime. Later, at Christmas, some childhood friends invite her to go skiing, and while with them she suffers an accident
and dies.

While there is some metaphorical elaboration, the narrative
aspects of the story are quite clear and the images, rather than dis-
tracting from the anecdotal content, serve to emphasize it. As in
"Hunter at Dawn," snow and winter have negative connotations
before the ideal of spring. There is much bird imagery, suggesting
the defenselessness of little Friaul and of Erika. The word "dirty" is
repeated with ominous insistence, casting a shadow over the
adolescence of Erika and her world.

José-Carlos Mainer points out that this selection is different from
Ayala's other vanguard creations of the same time in that it reveals
a historical moment of a concrete country. It was written in 1930
after Ayala had spent two years in Germany during the growth of
the Nazi movement. In his prologue to The Lamb's Head Ayala explains how a comment of the German Hispanist Walter Pabst made
him realize that even though his intention was basically aesthetic,
he had unintentionally reflected the tremendous and awesome
realities of those years. Ayala seems to endorse this viewpoint even
further by repeating the names of Erika's skiing friends—Trude and
Bruno—twenty-three years later in his story "La última cena"
("The Last Supper"). Here, they become German Jews who settle
in the Americas after suffering unspeakable horrors in Hitler's Germany. In view of the visionary quality of "Erika Facing Winter,"
one can only shudder in the face of the author's prophetic intuitions. Erika's consciousness that she belongs to the blond, blue-
eyed prototype separate from the Jews, her discomfort upon observing the homogeneity which winter garb imposes on the "herds" of
people, and the mutilated news story of the senseless killing of the
innocent child in front of the dumb, imploring stares of slaughtered
cattle in the butcher shop provide frightening premonitions of
future atrocities, make a convincing argument for the Surrealist
contention that the artist is ideally a prophet.

The search for Erika's friend Hermann, an attempt to reclaim
something from her age of innocence, becomes almost symbolic:

One never knows anything, ever! With the snows minds become mad, hands stir, knives sharpen, and God, dear God, refuses to intervene in the world!
Only a small and tender love can alleviate the winter. But in winter all doors are closed, all faces are unfriendly; and if perhaps, during a ride on a bus, some eyes defrosted and a mouth opened to declare: *My name is Hermann*, all this lasts only a moment . . . It's necessary to wait for spring to arrive, green with birds and accordions (447).

It is significant that the name Hermann resembles the Spanish word for brother, *hermano*. In Erika's frantic and frustrated search for her lost Hermann is her only hope for some sentiment which might be able to disperse the "dirty" clouds that darken the winter skies of her fatherland.

VI *Three Vanguard Parodies*

Although selections just discussed show the vanguard tendency to disparage myth, they also contain themes which are sufficiently serious to discourage calling them gratuitous. The author utilizes innovative techniques to treat his protagonists' encounters with destiny, adolescence, love and the absence of love. Three of his earliest stories (two of them from the book *The Boxer and an Angel*), however, appear to have as their fundamental inspiration the desire to parody respected traditions and to turn the sublime into the ridiculous.

In the Evangelical parody, "El gallo de la Pasión" ("St. Peter's Rooster"), dated 1927, Peter denies that he knows Christ; but when the resuscitated Lazarus, now in the form of a flaunting rooster, shoots three small arrows into him, he feels the sudden need for repentance. He asks the Roman soldiers to be excused as if it were a case of having to relieve urgent physical discomfort: "Excuse me, gentlemen. I have to leave for a moment. It's an absolute necessity. Excuse me, O.K.? Just a minute. I'll be right back" (398). Once in the street he does in fact relieve himself—by crying, "and—as was to be expected—God forgave him" (398). The humor injected by the suggestion of a physical necessity in a solemn moment of religious significance foreshadows later scenes in Ayala's fictions in which man's physical needs seem to crop up when he least expects, giving rise to ridiculous situations which underscore man's vulnerability.

"Susana saliendo del baño" ("Susan Leaving the Bath"), 1928, is a vanguard version of a well-known Biblical scene immortalized in paintings of "Susan in the Bath" by Veronese, Rembrandt, Rubens, Van Dyck, Mieris and Tintoretto. Ayala's interest in transmuting famous art works into banal reality is seen many years later in various selections of *The Garden of Delights,* 1971, where he includes photographs of the paintings and sculptures to which he refers. In the Bible, Susan, a chaste and beautiful Jewess, is spied upon by two lecherous old men who accuse her of adultery and are later sentenced to death for their calumny. Ayala's heroine is a latter-day Susan observed by two nickel faucets and admired by a smiling mirror, a sink, and a "round vegetal seat" in her bathroom. The author uses the movie techniques of slow motion and close-up as first the head, then a leg, a hand and finally the feet rise from the porcelain tub, described with striking and unusual metaphors. The presence of such an object as the round wooden seat of the commode serves to detract from the dignity of the scene and reminds us of the essential weakness of the human condition, tied to such ordinary and necessary functions.

"Medusa artificial" ("Artificial Medusa"), 1928, was published in the *Revista de Occidente* and presents a parody of the famous classical myth of Medusa and Perseus. The new Medusa is Mari Tere, a typist whose beautician Gabriel—complete with celestial smile and swinging doors as wings—gives her a permanent wave of curls twisted like reptiles, guaranteed "to turn men into stone." Her father Godofredo (Godfrey) drops his wine at the table—the first victim of his daughter's fatal hairdo—and before "the cry of the uncombed steam that the coffeepot exhaled," he avenges himself by the ceremonial wounding of a mannequin instead of imitating Perseus's decapitation of Medusa. There is some suggestion of the Electra myth in the sparks which the cables of the heroine's electric rollers emit. The use of both a chorus as in Greek tragedy and grandiloquent, religious subtitles of "Annunciation," "Martyrdom," and "Expiation" exaggerate the melodramatic effect the story is designed to elicit. They serve no visible purpose other than literary diversion—that is, the use of words and images to break with the past and to appeal to prevailing vanguard sensibilities.

CHAPTER 4

Historical "Examples":
Los usurpadores (The Usurpers)

THE intense unity apparent in the selections which compose *The Usurpers* belies the fact that they span some eleven years. The book was published in 1949, nineteen years after "Erika Facing Winter" appeared, and thus marks Ayala's renewal of the narrative genre following many years of silence, although in the interim he had published widely in the essay form. The earliest piece in the book is its epilogue, dated 1939, followed by "La campana de Huesca" ("The Bell of Huesca"), written in 1943. The last story, "El Inquisidor" ("The Inquisitor"), written in 1950, was added in a later edition.

With the cataclysms of the Spanish Civil War and World War II terminated at last, Ayala treats the problem of man's quest for power over his neighbor as a perennial one by situating his fictions in remote Spanish history where our vision is unobscured by direct reference to present-day circumstances. The prologue identifies these fictions as "examples," a word which immediately brings to mind the "exemplary novels" of Cervantes which our author has amply commented upon and interpreted as a scrutiny of moral values, involving the examination of motives, impulses and consequences which arouse intuitions in the reader and appeal to his conscience.[1] The writing of exemplary fiction implies an essential faith in man and in his ability to recognize and eventually correct his errors. It is important, however, to distinguish errors, followed by their immanent or perhaps inexorable consequences, from the moralistic concept of sin which calls for divine punishment in order to appreciate the posture of a writer of exemplary novels. The difference is most notable in the attitude of the novelist who, unlike the moralist who preaches a sermon, withdraws his presence, allowing the reader of his fictions to analyze and discover his own values by reading the text. So complete, in fact, is Ayala's absence in the pages of *The Usurpers* that it even extends to the prologue, supposedly written by a friend, and to the epilogue, offered by the dead in a desolate dialogue.

In view of the fact that these are Ayala's first stories written after a war which affected him personally and left him far from Spain, it is remarkable that instead of rendering direct testimony of terrible contemporary events, he was able to transmute them into historical fictions of a remote era with a perspective and vision that normally require great distance in time. It should also be noted that our author conceives of these "examples" as short novels rather than as "stories" because they are open-ended, ambiguous, and invite interpretation, while the "story" for Ayala is complete within itself and its sense is transparent.[2]

I   *Apocryphal Prologue*

One of Ayala's most extraordinary literary creations is his apocryphal prologue to *The Usurpers,* which is, in fact, an ingenious practical joke. The prologue purports to be written by "a newspaperman and archivist, at the request of the author, his friend" and is signed by F. de Paula A. G. Duarte. The prologuist was taken to be a real person by the critics until Ignacio Soldevila Durante and Keith Ellis revealed the full name of the author: Francisco de Paula Ayala García Duarte.[3] It became evident that this was a literary technique patterned after the Cervantine example of imaginative prologues and of self-fictionalization, as when reference is made to "a Spanish soldier named something Saavedra" (Miguel de Cervantes Saavedra).[4] It also recalls the manner in which Fernando de Rojas reveals his identity in an acrostic which follows a section entitled "The Author, to One, His Friend," preceding the text of *The Tragicomedy of Calisto and Melibea.*

The prologue, dated 1948, is identified as having been written in Coimbra, a city in Portugal, whose marginal location with regard to Spain reflects the situation of its author. Although Ayala has assured us that it is a coincidence, the word Coimbra is a very curious cryptograph whose value may be appreciated in the light of Surrealistic respect for the phenomenon of pure accident. The letters may be rearranged to read I. C. Broma. The Spanish names of the initials yield the word *hice* in phonetic writing, which combined with *broma,* Spanish for *joke,* provide the surprising confession that "the joke is mine."

The apocryphal prologue is invaluable for its explanation of the fictions which follow. Indeed, one of the hints as to the true identity of the obscure archivist of Coimbra is his uncanny literary insight. He explains that the underlying theme of the book is that "power exercised by one man over another is always a usurpation" and points out that interchangeable titles permit reshuffling, since there are numerous impostors, ailing leaders and brothers. He describes the advantage of treating historical material already exploited by other authors as it allows more attention to artistic elaboration and permits the reader to perceive intuitively analogies to present-day situations. The prologuist notes that the author's language, with its "moderate inflexion" of the times, is designed to suggest but not to imitate. He shows how the internal needs of each story determine its treatment, but refrains from discussing aesthetic values because of his "too close friendship with the author."

The clever fraud of a prologuist who, like other protagonists of *The Usurpers,* is also an "impostor," marks the marriage of irony with humor in Ayala's fictions, more profound than the playful metaphorical humor of his vanguard works. Here we have an inkling of the Ayala of *Historia de macacos (Monkey Story)* and his subsequent creations of masterful irony and humor.

Upon knowing the true identity of Duarte, statements which otherwise seem perplexing are greatly clarified and become humorous clues to the fraudulent nature of the prologue. Beneath the word "Prologue," for example, is a subtitle that sounds like that of a chapter of a novel, which we have already quoted, identifying the writer as an obscure newspaperman. As we read the prologue, we wonder why a friend of the author would characterize him as a "polygraph whose name appears in print perhaps too frequently" (453) or would censure his return to fiction after almost ten years of "dry sociological lucubrations" because it confuses his public image.[5] The prologuist's insistence on explaining things which he says are completely obvious is also suspicious. He calls our attention to details he considers "improbable" and "unbelievable," and finally concludes simplistically that spiritual health consists of "saintly resignation."

II   *"San Juan de Dios" ("St. John of God")*

"San Juan de Dios" can best be described as a short novel because of its complication and density. The point of departure is a picture of the saint which the narrator remembers from his childhood home and which inspires him to tell the story of the saint's conversion: Juan, a dissolute Portuguese soldier, was religiously inspired by a sermon of Juan de Avila in Granada and subsequently interned as a madman for his fanatical insistence upon confessing his sins publicly. He later founded a hospital for the poor. While begging in the streets, he was beaten by an impatient horseman and then helped by a boy and a wealthy lady who promised to support his cause of ministering to the sick and poor. Much later, when Juan is famous for his charity and piety, a gentleman seeks to ask his forgiveness for having beaten him, something he will never again do, for his hands have been horribly amputated. The man, whose name is Felipe Amor, tells Juan de Dios his story. He had managed to usurp the fortune of his cousin Fernando Amor and was going to marry Doña Elvira, whom his cousin had courted (and who, incidentally, is the same lady who had helped Juan de Dios). Fernando avenged himself by offending Doña Elvira with his hands, and for that reason, Felipe prepared a trap for him in which his hands would be amputated, but mistakenly, he fell victim to the same fate he had devised for the other. Juan de Dios effects a reconciliation and the two Amor cousins join him in his charitable works. When a plague attacks Granada, long wracked by civil strife, Fernando and Felipe are called to help Doña Elvira, whom they find already dead. Juan de Dios dies after many years of saintly dedication to the sick, and while the Amor cousins pray, we see the pious man in the same posture represented in the narrator's picture of the saint, recalled in the opening scene.

The story is framed very effectively by the repetition of the device of the immobile picture which opens and closes the narration as part of a childhood memory, making the content of the story seem very remote. Vertiginous changes of time—then, now, four hundred years ago, "my childhood," soon after, and years later—are expertly handled as they all fuse into a common violence. Ayala shows complete mastery of a technique which is constant in his later works: viewing the same occurrence from different perspectives; for example, the conversion of Juan de Dios is first summarized briefly by the narrator, later recounted as a legend, and finally described by Fernando Amor as something which impressed him profoundly.

Keith Ellis and Andrés Amorós have correctly pointed out antithesis as the dominant stylistic device used in the story, with its contrasts of horror and beauty, violence and piety, clear water under a dunghill, and a little gold cross in the midst of a plague. We must, however, go a step further and realize that these contrasts are means of achieving irony. The whole novelette is marked by a pervasive sense of irony right from the beginning when the narrator refers to his own life during the years in which the image of Juan de Dios has persisted in his mind: ". . . memorable events, unforeseen changes and horrible experiences, . . . mysteries, ambitions, hope, later ignominy and hate and forgiveness with its forgetting" (481), which are, in fact, all the elements which make up the story of Juan de Dios and the Amor cousins. The narrator's interest persists, though the personal subject "I" yields to the more general proof of the saint's fame: "They say." A subtle reference to "our Juan de Dios" suggests the exemplary nature of the saint, whose story belongs to the narrator, to us as readers, and to all of Spain.

The saddest irony is the unfortunate circumstance that violence must be the means of arriving at peace and reconciliation. This is shown individually in the case of Felipe Amor, whose name is in itself ironical, reduced physically to an almost animal condition by the loss of his hands, but inspired by this very misfortune to recover his human spirit. The warring cousins are described at the end as "brothers," which is significant in view of the fact that first cousins are called *primos hermanos* or "brother-cousins" in Spanish and the community founded by the saint is called "Brothers of San Juan de Dios." We see the moral renovation of individuals in Felipe and Fernando and in Juan de Dios, whose acts against God, whom he had denied, are expiated by self-mortification and acts of charity. The cousins' wrath and pride are directed against each other and must be corrected by mutual pardon. In all these examples, spiritual weakness is rectified, not by "saintly resignation," as the prologuist indicates, but rather, as the narrator states, by "pious heroism."

There is, on the other hand, a lack of moral renovation in society as a whole in the incessant repetition of violence in Granada: first the Moorish civil wars before the time of Juan, the Morisco rebellion years later, and the affliction of plagues, which like wars, join enemies in common graves. The imploration of the saint in the midst of the plague "sent by Heaven" which competes with civil strife for bodies, is significant: "How much longer, Lord?"

As we have indicated, there is an accumulation of ironical circumstances throughout this short novel. The hands that offended the living woman prepare her shroud. The plague of man's violence and the plague itself are described in very explicit and repugnant terms, while a mere verbal interjection deemed objectionable in the mouth of a young boy is eluded in a footnote by the author. There is irony, too, in the aura of Juan's saintliness which comes post-humously in the attribution of the "miracles" of a strange light in the sky and bells ringing by themselves at his birth, as if miracles were more essential than virtue.

III   "El doliente" ("The Ailing King")

"The Ailing King" (1946) is set in the city of Burgos, beginning as Enrique III, (king of Castile from 1390 to 1406), hears his huntsman arrive. He is attended only by his silent demented nursemaid, whose mental deterioration has paralleled Enrique's own illness which has made him unable to exercise his authority. The power is being usurped by the nobles, led by the bishop, who wish to dismember the kingdom. The ailing King Enrique recovers sufficiently to plan a clever trap by feigning extreme illness and assembling all the nobles to hear his last will and testament. Thus the king's guards are able to disarm and arrest them, and Enrique, exhausted by the experience, is also disarmed, undressed and put to bed by his servants. A sudden transition to autumn presents the king awakening from fevers and delirium, bewildered upon lear-ning that he himself had decreed the release of his enemies.

In sharp contrast to the ailing king, frustrated and foiled by his illness, his wet-nurse's idiot son, Enrique González, is ironically full of boundless energy wasted in useless activities. A story within the story, recounted in the kitchen by a servant, tells of a grand feast given by Bishop Ildefonso, whose extravagance contrasts with the extreme poverty in the palace. The gluttony of the nobles is des-cribed as a prelude to that of their hearts, since they prepare to cut up the kingdom and devour it. The greed of the prelate is graphical-ly communicated by two anecdotes. First of all, pale and perspiring, he had to leave the banquet in order to make a quick exit to his chambers, obviously to relieve himself of great physical discomfort caused by overeating. The blacksmith tells how three years before, the bishop also had to run from the altar during mass. This incident was much more serious, since he was supposed to be fasting. These anecdotes, repeated in the banal atmosphere of the palace kitchen, relax the tension of the rest of the novel and provide a humorous in-terlude, not without significance, for the bishop is symbolically con-trasted with the king: The first is unable to control his excesses, the other his weaknesses.

The readers' compassion is invited by the servant who laments the captive state of his "poor master." We realize from the king's monologues how limited he is by his ailment, which prevents him from bearing the responsibility of power, for this responsibility is abused as equally by weakness as by excess. As his huntsman aptly puts it: "Sir, if you, the king, abandon your people, how can you expect your vassals not to abandon you" (485), for even the king's dog leaves him to sniff at some food.

The first scenes are slow motion close-ups of the ailing king's dry lips, eyelids, pupils, and folded hands, as we witness his frustrated attempts to raise himself and to obtain answers from his silent nursemaid, and his confusion about time as he tries to straighten out his "shuffled thoughts." Then there is an ascending movement as he seems to recover somewhat and take charge of the situation by pawning his cape to provide food in the palace and planning the climactic entrapment of the nobles. The reader is as surprised as the forsaken monarch to find the nobles free. While we sympathize with his unfortunate plight, we cannot help but wonder at the enigma which the king had posed to the nobles: Which is worse, successive reigns of five very different autocrats or the simultaneous anarchy of five or even twenty? The latter is the situation resulting from the complete absence of centralized power in the kingdom, which is as catastrophic as despotism.

IV   *"La campana de Huesca" ("The Bell of Huesca")*

This story, whose title refers to the form in which the heads of all the nobles of Huesca were placed in the atrium of the church, is based on an "uncertain legend" of events which occurred in 1136, also treated in literary works by the nineteenth-century writers Manuel Fernández y González and Cánovas de Castillo.

As in "San Juan de Dios," the beginning and end are related, providing a sort of frame for the story. The plot is summarized first, in the medieval manner, so that the reader can concentrate on the details and artistic elaboration: "In those times when a man knew how to make dignity of service and service of life, because he lived for death, a monk of royal blood was taken from the devotion in which he lived absorbed and was elevated among men to occupy the throne" (501). Following this preliminary summary, is the detailed story of Ramiro the Monk, who found a destiny of submission imposed upon him by birth, as second royal son. Renouncing this subservient position "created to vilify the vile, making him wallow in his vileness" (502), and abhorring power, he learns to use his own strength to dominate all ambition and impose meekness upon himself. Throughout the story the dominant force of his proud royal blood tries to break forth as he exerts all his power to contain it.

The will of King Alfonso, however, has left the throne to the military orders so that his power and authority will die with him, and in the absence of other heirs, Ramiro accepts the reign as an obligation and part of his "true" destiny. He submits to marriage, but mortifies himself to suppress love and passion. He fulfills what he considers his duty by engendering an heir and then beheading all the magnates—beginning with the prelate of Huesca who, counting on his meekness, had recalled him to the throne. Thus he who "feared his own power more than his subjects did" (508) adopts the homeopathic remedy of alleviating his fear of power by exercising it violently, only to surrender it willingly to the twenty-four-year-old future husband of his two-year-old daughter. The last seventeen years of his life are spent, ironically, carrying out his original destiny of "living in the Court in the dignity without service that corresponded to the order of his birth" (512) as second born. In this story, too, the narrator poses an enigma before the example of Ramiro, whose "false" destiny becomes a "true" one as he retains the empty title of king: "Who really knows his own destiny?" (501).

The narrator, who tells the story with a "vague air of chronicle" according to the prologuist, eliminates the use of dialogue and interior monologue or introspection that might humanize his character or provide explanations of his actions. The power is in the hands of a rather impassive omniscient narrator who describes even the most repugnant scenes, such as the actual birth of the princess—which Ramiro himself witnesses—and the sight of a dog licking the blood of a headless trunk, with the same coolness with which his protagonist acts. His matter-of-fact attribution of Ramiro's execution of the nobles to the inevitable forces of blood, destiny and divine illumination give the story a distinctly medieval tone.

V   *"Los impostores"* (*"The Impostors"*)

"The Impostors," 1947, is based on the historical theme of the young king of Portugal's suicidal expedition against Morocco in

1568 and the subsequent power void which brought the country under the rule of Spain, creating popular expectations which gave rise to numerous fraudulent attempts to reclaim the Portuguese crown, left vacant by the king's disappearance. Ayala retells the story of an impostor who previously was the subject of another famous literary work, José Zorrilla's romantic drama of 1849, *Traidor, inconfeso y mártir (Unconfessed Traitor and Martyr)*, in which the "Pastryman of Madrigal," hanged for treason as an impostor, really is the lost King Don Sebastián.

As we have seen in previous selections from *The Usurpers*, Ayala sums up the plot beforehand by telling us that the pretender to Don Sebastián's crown found that the steps of the throne turned into those of the scaffold. The reader is given the role of witness as Don Sebastián's old confessor is heard exhorting the hopeful pretender whose cause he has espoused to measure up to the responsibility he seeks. He brings him before Princess Ana who offers him her obedience and her jewels, and impressed by these symbols of power, the young man becomes exalted.

A surprise awaits the reader, however, when the confessor alarmed at the "impetuous majesty" of "the king" in his handling of the nobles, and at the "truth of his lie," is reminded of the same trait which caused the loss of Portugal twenty years before. While the prelate listens to Doña Ana's own expression of doubt with regard to the authenticity of the pretender, the latter is taken prisoner and hanged.

The fact that the characters express themselves predominantly in form of dialogue, in the absence of substantial narrative explanation, prevents the reader from perceiving clearly the machinations of the intrigue, making it necessary to conjecture about a number of puzzling questions. There is doubt as to the exact patriotic or personal motives (recalling "The Bell of Huesca," in which the prelate who brought Ramiro to power was his first victim) of the fearful confessor in betraying his overzealous candidate, the degree of innocence or malice on the part of the impostor, and the meaning of the facial gesture directed to his mother who is brought "flying in the air" like a witch to witness his hanging.

Subtle hints of the confessor's deception appear early in the story when he falls into a chair "enervated like a puppet in a fair, after the show" (519), remarkably similar to the final view of the victim hanging from the scaffold like a loose rag doll, prompting the narrator's comment that "one would have said that the whole scene

had been nothing more than a poor practical joke played by village
players" (529). The prelate was just as much an impostor as the
pastryman he supported: two actors in an empty drama.

Ayala provides an important comment in his prologue, stating
that the pastryman was *bewitched* by power (hence the presenta-
tion of his mother as a witch), just as the demoniacal Don Sebastián
was in his irrational undertakings. The fate of the ill-starred king, as
well as that of his impostor are summarized at the beginning of the
story, emphasizing the similarities between them, for the fall of Don
Sebastián's star in a pool of blood is very much like that of the
pastryman from proud heights to the darkness of the dungeon and
death. The confessor's speech to his candidate is essentially true:
"Identity, sir, is more a matter of the soul than of the body" (516),
but he finds with dismay that power and its attraction may create
identities all too similar. The impostor's last exclamation: "Poor
Don Sebastián, what have you come to?," underscores the degree to
which his ambition actually transformed him into the man whose
role he was designed to act.

VI   *"El Hechizado"* (*"The Bewitched"*)

When it was first published in 1944, "The Bewitched" was
characterized as "one of the most memorable stories of Hispanic
literature" by the venerable Argentine man of letters Jorge Luis
Borges.[6] José Marra-López considered it the most perfect narration
in *The Usurpers*, an opinion which other critics share.[7] It is a
masterpiece whose chief merit resides in a carefully elaborated
structure which reflects perfectly its content.

In "The Bewitched" a scholarly narrator transcribes the
manuscript of the Indian González Lobo, who made a trip from his
native Andes to Spain in order to gain access to the presence of
King Carlos II, who was called "the Bewitched," but who was really
an imbecile. As the prologuist points out, the structure of the story
conducts the reader through its labyrinths from the uncomplicated
Andean setting of its beginnings to the void at the center of power,
where González Lobo discovers the "skeleton of an old bureaucratic
State" (455) in the person of the decadent remnant of what was
once a powerful dynasty.

The narrator, as in other selections in *The Usurpers*, functions to
set a frame for González Lobo's chronicle which begins in the
Andes in 1679 and is written in America in his old age when "faint
echoes of the civil war awaken neither his emotion nor curiosity."

This statement is particularly ironic in view of Ayala's own experience with a Spanish Civil War. Within the frame of the chronicle, there is another frame: the wedding of Carlos II at the outset of González Lobo's voyage, and later his death, causing the civil war which ensues. With little regard for order, the narrator transcribes the manuscript, criticizing its writer's penchant for repetition, emphasis on trivialities, silence regarding his personal affairs, and lack of emotion and originality. He asks what reason González Lobo had for writing the manuscript, and the reader finds himself asking the same question about the transcriber, who is guilty of the same disconcerting handling of incidents that he criticizes, and which, by the way, characterizes Ayala's own style of writing!

The prologue tells us that González Lobo is as bewitched as the king he seeks, for he carries out "with probity the task which he has imposed on himself—transcribing the entire manuscript from start to finish, line by line, not omitting even a period" (538). There are, then, several labyrinths: the senseless ceremonies of an empty state, a trip that seems purposeless, a manuscript recording the trip in minute detail, and an absurd scholarly dedication to such a manuscript. All these labyrinths are characterized by interminable papers, folders and ink. As in the *Quijote*, there is great uncertainty with regard to truth and fiction: The transcriber suspects that the manuscript may be fictitious; he himself is fictitious, and the story is commented upon by a prologuist invented by the author Ayala.

While the language itself is clear and uncomplicated, the stucture and perspectives are extremely baroque, as though mirrors were reflecting mirrors, reducing objects until they are barely visible. Slow motion and close-ups create a diminishing perspective so that the climactic view of His Majesty, drooling on his velvet clothes, whose stench reveals that he cannot control his bodily functions, much less an empire, appears in the tiny perspective befitting such a character. The enormous bureaucratic structure of officials, foreigners and servants, as well as endless hallways, staircases and galleries lead to what Marra-López describes as the "faraway, supreme ruler, the diminutive point way up at the top."[8] His terminology is exact, for the king sits in a huge chair among his subjects: a dwarf, a tiny dog and a little monkey. The reader, who like González Lobo, must find his way through a massive labyrinth, finally gains access to the king's chamber, only to find a one-paragraph description of the hapless head of a vast microcephalic empire, and a sudden and abrupt end to the story.

VII   *"El Inquisidor"* (*"The Inquisitor"*)

This short novel is undoubtedly one of Ayala's best achievements
in the narrative genre. Published separately in 1950, it was later included in *The Usurpers,* originally published the year before,
because it corresponds to the times and tone of other works in that
collection, and treats an analogous theme.

When the story opens, the Great Rabbi of the Jewish quarter of a
"small city in the Castilian plain" (this ambiguity is very Cervantine), having converted to Catholicism, laments the persistence
among his people of fifteen centuries of error. We see him again
eight years later as Bishop-Inquisitor, attempting to compensate for
his past and redeem his ancestors by his extreme zeal. He has spent
a difficult night of reflection which has resulted in a death sentence
that will end three-year-old proceedings against his own brother-in-
law, Antonio María Lucero, a convert imprisoned on the suspicion
of being an insincere Christian. The Inquisitor mentally reviews the
scene of Lucero's torture satisfied that he alone was capable of
noting that under torture the accused had invoked God, but not
Jesus, the Virgin, or the saints, to whom he had shown great devotion in less trying circumstances. The Inquisitor recalls the eyes that
glowed from the floor in the darkness where the accused was tied by
his ankles upside down. Marta, the Inquisitor's beloved daughter,
had intervened in his favor, an act which angered her father and led
him to dismiss her tutor, an "Old Christian" (as opposed to a convert). The solitary prelate also thinks of his grandfather's brother,
who became an insincere Moslem convert and as muezzin of a
mosque scoffed at the Moors by execrating Mohammed in Hebrew
words interpolated in the Arabic prayers. The Inquisitor reviews the
endless folios and denunciations before him, recalling disturbing
dreams in which he was in the place of both the false muezzin and
Lucero.

In the morning, his secretary and daughter enter. Marta
reproaches her father for arresting her tutor and condemns his
fanaticism, warning him that the Son of God may be among those
he arrests and tortures each day. She finally challenges him: "You
won't arrest me because I'm your daughter. You would burn alive
the Messiah himself!" (137). The Bishop, with a gesture expected
by his secretary, decrees proceedings against his daughter, imploring: "Help me, Father Abraham!"

The reference to Abraham in this hour of tribulation is, of course, tremendously significant, for the patriarch was also faced with the sacrifice of his child as a proof of faith. This Old Testament sacrifice, however, was aborted, while in the New Testament a similar sacrifice in the name of redemption is consummated with a new theological meaning in the crucifixion. As readers, we do not know whether the Inquisitor has realized the ultimate meaning of his exclamation, since he is obviously guilty of the same *lapsus* or slip of the tongue he condemned in Lucero. As we, the readers, assume the role of Inquisitor, Marta's quote from the Gospel serves as an admonishment that goes far beyond her father, to whom it was directed: "Judge not others, lest ye be judged."

The symbolical use of light is skillfully incorporated into the texture of the novel. The eyes of Lucero, whose very name means light or bright star, shine at the Inquisitor in the darkness in an accusing fashion. Both are insecure in their new faith; the only difference between them is caused by their respective positions of power (up or down as when Lucero's viewpoint is from below and the Inquisitor's is from above, or when the situation is reversed as in the dream). With regard to the prelate's conversion, it is specified that he "recognized the light of the truth" (545), but ironically, his eyes are nearsighted and confuse Lucero with Lucifer. A detailed description is given of all the objects that surround the Inquisitor, but there is no mention of a candle or any other light illuminating the darkness in which he works, while it is noted that a small lamp provides light in Marta's room.

With regard to possible sources of "The Inquisitor," Andrés Amorós, in his introduction to the 1970 edition of *The Usurpers*, reminds us that the first two Inquisitors were converts: Tomás de Torquemada and Brother Diego de Deza. Ayala, in answer to a query from Hugo Rodríguez Alcalá, provides the example of Pablo de Santa María, a rabbi who later became a bishop.[9] Rodríguez-Alcalá sees a similarity in Ayala's rendering of the Inquisitor to that of El Greco's painting of Fernando Niño de Guevara, of 1600.[10] This observation seems to be confirmed by an article Ayala published in *La Nación* and in *Diálogos* in 1974, entitled "Inquisidor y rabino" ("Inquisitor and Rabbi"), in which he tells of his astonishment upon running into the Inquisitor General Fernando Niño de Guevara near his apartment in New York, escaped from El Greco's portrait, and now dressed as a rabbi!

Literary precedents may also be cited, for two years before Ayala's story was published, Azorín's brief piece "The Old Inquisitor," appearing in his work *Una hora de España (entre 1560 y 1570) (An Hour of Spain [Between 1560 and 1570])*, presented an Inquisitor faced with the decision of accusing his only son who is guilty of bringing prohibited books from Paris. It is even more inconclusive than Ayala's story, since Azorín leaves us in suspense about the Inquisitor's final determination as his son's hand slowly turns the knob of the door which leads to his father's chamber.

A fact that has not been noted, even though "The Inquisitor" is one of Ayala's most celebrated writings, is its similarity to "The Grand Inquisitor" interpolated by Dostoevsky in his novel *The Brothers Karamazov*. Here, too, we see not only the implacable rigor of a fearful prelate victimized by a terrible personal secret that makes him as tortured and guilty as those he condemns (his religious disbelief), but also an innocent condemned to die (Christ himself, as Marta suggests in Ayala's story). In both works, the center of interest is the solitary and tragic man who exercises temporal power based on spiritual power, and since they serve a system, they remain nameless. It should be noted that our author's admiration for Dostoevsky, and specifically for *The Brothers Karamazov*, is expressed in his essay on "El arte de novelar y el oficio del novelista" ("The Art of Writing Novels and the Work of a Novelist"), written in 1955.

Ayala's basic theme, as well as Dostoevsky's, is the prostitution of freedom and the horror of justifying violence in the name of God. The Inquisitor usurps others' freedom requiring of them even subconscious faith, but when he experiences torture (mental, not physical, like Lucero's), his own subconscious betrays his essential insecurity. Ayala provides a valuable key to this situation in his essay "La perspectiva hispánica" ("The Hispanic Perspective") in his book *Razón del mundo (The World Explained,* 1944): The fanaticism of the persecutor covers up his own doubt and eases his trembling conscience.

VIII   *"El abrazo" ("The Embrace")*

Presented from the point of view of an old and trusted counselor, "The Embrace" involves the reign of Pedro "the Cruel" in the fourteenth century, beleaguered by his illegitimate half-brothers. The story begins with old Juan Alfonso's taking leave of Castile to escape the wrath of Don Enrique, the half-brother who has killed Pedro and usurped the throne.

With great technical skill, the author achieves dramatic effects by contrasting intimate moments, which invite the reader's sympathy toward the plight of the characters, with other scenes in which these same characters exercise a violence that is not only monstrous, but is seemingly beyond their control. Our compassion for the queen mother who has suffered for twenty-eight years while another woman has usurped her place in the heart of King Alfonso, is transformed into disgust when she enacts her vengeance. In this grizzly scene, we feel little sympathy as she gloats over the severed head of the rival she ordered killed. Her son Pedro's acquiescence to his tutor's advice to seek reconciliation, and his tender dialogue with his beloved concubine María provide a marked contrast to the volatile temper and lack of restraint which precipitate the assassination of one half-brother and finally his own death at the hands of another. At the same time, he often employs his ire in just causes, and even the French princess who was brought to the court to marry this man who ignores her completely, has more complaints about the court than about him personally. Pedro's tragedy is that to him the word brother means enemy, the horror of which is underscored by the fact that he recognizes some of his own features in the face of his half-brother Fadrique, brutally murdered on his orders. The protective embrace of María contrasts with the epic scene of the fratricidal embrace of death which marks Pedro's only face-to-face meeting with Don Enrique, arranged by well-intentioned intermediaries who are anxious to terminate so many years of strife.

The old tutor's discretion, prudence, and good intentions come to naught, as do other sporadic efforts to bring peace to the warring family. Like the game of chess which Pedro destroys in order not to lose, all the brothers—legitimate and illegitimate—are pawns in some inexorable destiny which they help along with their personal crimes and public atrocities. From this interminable chain of violence, the only escape is flight. The poor young princess flees to France, where she asks her father "Why?" There seems to be neither an answer nor a solution, and Pedro's old tutor Juan Alfonso, just like Francisco Ayala in real life, takes sad leave of his "land of salt and iron" wracked by fratricidal conflict.

IX   *"Diálogo de los muertos"* (*"Dialogue of the Dead"*)

In this selection Ayala employs the dialogue form which he had used in a limited fashion in *Tale of a Dawn* and which he uses for satirical purposes years later in his "Diálogos de amor" ("Dialogues of Love"). As Rosario Hiriart explains, the "dialogue of the dead" is a genre originating with Lucian and quite common in medieval French literature.[11]Ayala combines this form with the tone of the traditional medieval "Dance of Death," from which he extracts a brief quote.

In this desolate dialogue, the interred, anonymous dead comment about the living and reveal compassion for them. All of the living—the violent as well as the weak—are in fact dead, for like animals, they are ignorant of their destiny. Their only ray of hope is that they can review the past and retrace the road traveled, whereas the dead, who have no future, cannot.

Keith Ellis suggests the influence of T. S. Eliot and Jean Paul Sartre in certain passages. There are, however, Spanish counterparts to Ayala's bleak vision such as Quevedo's famous poem (studied by Ayala) "How All Things Speak of Death," which leads from the walls of his country in ruins to his own personal desolation, and Mariano José de Larra's famous essay "The Day of the Dead, 1836," characterizing all Madrid as a vast cemetery. With an irony akin to Ayala's, Larra remarks that those who visit the cemetery to honor the dead are as dead as those they visit, and worse off since those they buried are free.

Ayala's "Dialogue of the Dead" which closes *The Usurpers*, forms a sort of epilogue which in fact alludes to all the themes developed in the stories which the volume comprises, but since it precedes all of them chronologically, it may be the seedplot from which they germinated. The subtitle "Spanish Elegy" connects the remote historical examples of *The Usurpers* to the present as implicit comments on the Civil War.

X   *A Biblical Postscript*

Although Ayala's story "El loco de fe y el pecador" ("The Frantic Believer and the Sinner") was never included in *The Usurpers*, undoubtedly because its setting is not Spanish, it belongs to the same era (1942) and represents the same creative vein. His reworking of Biblical material here is reminiscent of his earlier vanguard works "Saint Peter's Rooster" and "Susan Leaving the Bath," also treating such themes.

The beginning of the story sounds more like an essay purporting to explain parables never told or only partially presented in the Gospels. The first parable is about a blind believer who comes too late and mistakes the traitor for the already crucified healer. His faith is so great that when the sinner accidently brushes his eyes in piety and terror, his vision is restored. This example of literally "blind faith" which benefits both the believer and the sinner, by moving the latter to repentance, provides the background for a different version of the "Prodigal Son," who returns to those from whom he fled, overcoming the hatred of his origin through love. Rather than being a parable of paternal pardon, it is one of a son who triumphs over his repulsion for his own blood. The paradoxical birth of love from hatred (reminding us of similar paradoxes in the works of Miguel de Unamuno) extends to the awakening of love and pardon both in the man who kills his brother and in his victim. The reader may note that these same ideas inspire "San Juan de Dios" and "Dialogue of the Dead."

CHAPTER 5

Civil War in Men's Hearts: La cabeza del cordero (The Lamb's Head)

A S we have seen, Ayala's concern with the Spanish Civil War of 1936 is transmuted into historical examples in *The Usurpers.* He approaches the actual period of the conflict in *The Lamb's Head,* published later in the same year, 1949, but these are not war stories. As the author explains in his proem, the same anguish which inspired *The Usurpers* provides the impulse for this volume in which he examines the theme of "the civil war in men's hearts" and portrays the permanent aspects of the passions that feed such wars.

The author's proem is one of his most revealing documents about the experience of the Spanish Civil War and its impact on his works. Ayala discusses the situation of Spanish letters before the war and after the "great crisis of the Occident" (600).[1] He describes his generation, with few exceptions, as a "cemetery of promises" and comments upon the evasion of the theme of the Civil War in Spain, despite its being the "central experience of my generation" (602). Because of the "irregular" situation, he feels obligated to help orient the reader and clarify circumstances and attitudes. We find that his approach is basically moral and not political or anecdotal. Ayala states his purpose clearly: he wishes to portray the "guilty-innocent or the innocent-guilty," sound the abyss of inhumanity, purge the heart, and show evil for what it is so that it may be annihilated. The conditions of a world out of order demand his dedication to such a task.

Ayala's confessions in *The Lamb's Head* represent the conclusions of a writer of conscience who has lowered himself into his own personal inferno of experience. While the stories themselves are inventions, the passions they depict are unfortunately real. Perhaps for this reason, there is so much insistence on the truth of what is described; "The Message" begins with the words: "Let the truth be told," and in "One's Life for Reputation," the narrator admonishes: "These aren't stories." At the same time, however, our attention is called to events which are described as unbelievable and novel, as if to warn us that the terms "truth" and "fiction" are never absolutes, especially when literary invention serves as a means of discovering truth.

Particularly noteworthy is the balance Ayala achieves in distributing credit and blame to individuals of both sides. With the possible exception of the last story, added years after the original edition of 1949, there is little to show that Ayala wrote from a position of self-exile in America. Each protagonist is convincing and acquires his own personality, carrying within him the seeds of conflict or reconciliation, often not realizing his own weaknesses even though he may sound the very confines of his soul. This is communicated by the expert handling of first-person narration in all of the stories except "The Tagus," where the protagonist is observed by an outside narrator. Further significance may be attributed to the constant use of first-person by narrators who are egotistical and who have an extremely limited capacity for humane feelings.

I   *"El mensaje"* (*"The Message"*)

In "The Message," 1948, the narrator tells about his visit to his cousin Severiano, whom he had not seen for eight years. He tries to impress his cousin, a small-town dealer in agricultural equipment, with his travels and exaggerates his knowledge of languages, feeling immensely superior to the country bumpkins who consume their lives in "mediocrity." Severiano consults him about deciphering a paper which was left in the town's inn by a mysterious stranger who disappeared the next day. Ironically, everyone can repeat exactly what the man ate, but cannot offer a description of him. The paper, which no one can read, incites discussions, arguments and resentment among the townspeople and within Severiano's own family. Intrigued by the story, irritated by his country cousin, and unable to sleep, the narrator insists on seeing the paper which he believes is a coded message. The custodian of the note, Severiano's old maid sister Juanita, explodes in a tirade of insults, flinging the key at them so they can invade her desk and "destroy everything." The narrator is perplexed when nothing is found and puzzled even more by the complete indifference of his cousin.

Andrés Amorós likens this story to "The Bewitched," a very appropriate analogy since everyone is bewitched by the incomprehensible message, and after a bewildering search through a labyrinth of details, the results are disappointing.[2] Ayala explains in his proem that the message announces the Civil War, which is not to say that this is the deciphered content of the paper, but rather its impact. Juanita's desk is a sort of Pandora's box from which the evil has already escaped to occupy the hearts of the Spanish people. Routine and boredom give rise to obsessions, which are the raw materials of war, but so are feelings of superiority, vanity, and envy, like those apparent in the narrator, although he is incapable of seeing his own faults. The first-person narrative effectively convinces the reader of his limited, self-centered perspective.

Besides providing a picture of the atmosphere of Spanish people on the brink of crisis, "The Message" is a good mystery story since the reader is as confused and fascinated as the narrator; at the end, both wonder if the message ever really existed. Maybe the whole story was an invention of Severiano's to entertain his "worldly" cousin, taking advantage of the madness of Juanita who "since becoming a devout old maid feeds her imagination with stupid fantasies and likes to use words like *message, mission, holocaust*" (626).

II *"El Tajo"* (*"The Tagus"*)

The title of this story, written in 1949, is a pun on the name of the river which passes through Toledo, scene of part of the action but which also means "incision," suggesting the schism which the Civil War caused in Spanish society.

The story begins with the account of what turned out to be the only memorable event of the war for Lieutenant Santolalla, a native of Toledo. While picking grapes in a vineyard in the quiet Aragon front, he surprises and kills an enemy militiaman who, like himself, was gathering grapes. His thoughts later wander to the past, to scenes which seem to have no direct relation to what happened in Aragon, but which trouble his conscience and stimulate feelings of guilt. He remembers family debates arising from partisan sympathies of the First World War, the remote innocent world of infancy when he walked with his mother in a garden, his indignation at the beating of a washerwoman by her drunken husband, the killing of his dog Chispa by some heartless person, and his intense feelings of hatred, frustration, and desire for revenge when a neighbor boy threw dung at him. All of these memories, with the

presence of violence and helpless victims, are of course subconscious associations incited by Santolalla's act of violence in
Aragon.

After the war, Santolalla returns to Toledo where his family was
fortunately able to return to normal because his brother-in-law and
grandfather were among the victorious Nationalists. A few years
later, he attempts to alleviate his feelings of guilt by returning the
papers of his victim to his impoverished family in Toledo and by
offering his help. To Santolalla's surprise, the mother, suspicious of
this alleged "friend" of her son's who seems to have fared too well
while her husband and other son were tortured and killed "like rab-
bits," rejects both the papers and his help. Obviously, a socialist
identification card would only serve to incriminate and compromise
what is left of her family.

Santolalla, like the old tutor Juan Alfonso of "The Embrace," is
understanding and well-intentioned but helpless before the schism
of civil strife. There is symbolism in the emphasis given to the
stench of the dead man, and later to that of the dog Chispa,
suggesting the malodorous, offensive nature of war which in other
references is a disease accompanied by the sensations of vertigo and
nausea. It is ironic that Santolalla's crime, committed on the impulse of fear, takes place in the peacefulness of the Aragonese front
when it is stressed that atrocities were occurring in cities like
Madrid and Toledo. The peaceful Garden of Eden of his childhood
is changed by the break in Spanish society into a vineyard defiled
by the crime of Cain. There is also great irony in the relief of the
Republican militiaman's mother upon learning that her son did not
die like a rabbit as the other men of the family did, for indeed his
death was that of a helpless animal stalked while feeding.

"The Tagus" is Ayala's only story set in the midst of the war. In
view of his personal circumstances, Ayala succeeds in representing
without bias the fear which causes a man to kill his neighbor and a
mother to renounce her son. He implies that it is of little importance to invoke political causes when suffering seems equally dis-
tributed among a sensitive victor and the survivors of the victims.

III *"El regreso" ("The Return")*

"The Return," 1948, is very similar to "The Bewitched" in *The
Usurpers* in that the protagonist leaves America (Buenos Aires) on a
trip to Spain (his native Galicia) where he finds himself in a
labyrinth, and then returns again to America. Upon his arrival in

Galicia, his aunt informs him that soon after he had disappeared, his childhood friend Abeledo had led a group of Nationalists or Falangists to arrest him. The narrator reflects on his past relationships with Abeledo in search of motives for the betrayal, asking himself whether he would have done the same if the circumstances had been reversed. With fear and anxiety, he tries to find Abeledo in a labyrinth that extends from his aunt's house through the streets of Santiago to the barbershop, the café, Abeledo's former house, and finally to a brothel where he is shocked to find Abeledo's sister, ironically named María Jesús. He had never been able to think of her romantically in spite of his friend's obvious efforts to align them because she looked too much like her brother. As in "The Bewitched" and "The Message," the center of the labyrinth is empty since Abeledo has been killed. The narrator feels drawn to María Jesús and realizes how much he had meant to this "poor creature" (703); however, in the epilogue, he laments the time lost in search of Abeledo and the "sordid" meeting with "that damned María Jesús" (704). After a visit to Abeledo's grave, he returns to Buenos Aires which adds still another "return" to the title.

The narrator impresses us as generally unfeeling, especially toward women, evidenced in the contempt he shows for the girl friend he left abruptly in America, his aunt, and María Jesús. His compassion, a departure from his usual character as a rather brutal man, is for this reason especially moving since he comes to grips with his conscience via the sister of his enemy-friend. The significance of his union with María Jesús in the brothel has not been considered by the critics, but it is, in fact, a vicarious reconciliation with his enemy since it is stressed that an excessive resemblance between the girl and her brother had always made him feel uneasy. The same person who might have provided an unbreakable link between the friends if the narrator had accepted marriage became instead the motive of Abeledo's revengeful betrayal. The narrator jokingly describes María Jesús as dove-breasted, suggesting to the reader the image of the peace dove, for now that Abeledo is dead, she is an instrument of reconciliation, as it were.

Throughout the story we can see how the atmosphere of the Civil War fosters discord between brother and sister and friends, turning Abel into a Cain who uses the war to satisfy personal vendettas.

Symbolism may be seen in the prostitution of María Jesús, whose name suggests innocence, for wars prostitute many values such as friendship and loyalty. Times, circumstances, and people change, and the narrator, now overcome by enervation and boredom, finds it hard to recognize in himself a once enthusiastic and zealous patriot. He cannot understand the changes which occurred in Abeledo, but he himself is given to abrupt changes of mood toward others, shifting suddenly from humane concern to complete lack of feeling.

Since the first-person narrative limits us to the information which the narrator wishes to give, the reader cannot know to what extent motives attributed to Abeledo are exact. We are confronted by the same ambiguity and confusion that marked the Civil War in which it was not always possible to distinguish friend from foe. As Abeledo's epitaph reveals, the traitor was himself betrayed by unknown assassins. The narrator's obsessive quest for Abeledo is in itself an extension of Civil War passions, still capable of inciting possibly another "return" to violence if not halted first by reconciliation. His trip, which he characterizes as a descent into a brothel-inferno, has the quality of a nightmare from which he emerges somewhat purged and eager to escape. Like the stories of Spanish atrocities he had heard while in America, his own experience seems unreal.

IV   *"La cabeza del cordero"* ("*The Lamb's Head*")

José Torres, narrator of "The Lamb's Head," 1948, explains that while he was on business in Fez a messenger approached him and led him to a Moorish Torres family claiming to be relatives separated from the Spanish branch of the family centuries ago by the Morisco expulsion. His conversations with these Moorish relatives, at first an entertaining adventure, awaken in his memory unpleasant scenes from his own family's past related to the Civil War. He cannot blot out the picture of his uncle Jesús's unclaimed body, for he refused to identify it in order to protect himself. Furthermore, he had later used the case of his uncle killed by the "Reds" as proof of his allegiance to the Nationalists. He convinces himself that he could not have prevented Jesús's murder or his uncle Manuel's plight which resulted in exile in America. He tells his young Moorish "cousin" Yusuf about his cousin Gabrielillo, chosen by lots to be killed for drawing a hammer and sickle on the walls of his Nationalist prison. José feels more and more uneasy as he joins his new-found family for a dinner which also implies bloodshed: carmine marmelade made from roses and cold lamb with the animal's severed head split wide open in the center of the platter, causing a night of insomnia and indigestion. He finally vomits to relieve the distress that the lamb's head produces in his stomach, and the next day he leaves Fez, shaken at seeing the Moorish family's messenger alongside his bus.

The dizziness, vertigo, and nausea of the narrator is not the metaphysical nausea of Sartre, but rather a moral indigestion produced by repressed guilt. José Torres's sudden confrontation with a branch of his family, long since expelled by old civil wars, stirs his conscience to recognize his own responsibility in the latest war which he had evaded to save his own skin. He is disarmed by his Moorish aunt's affection because he had divested himself of his family ties in denying his uncle Jesús. He is also impressed by the story of Torres, the Evader (like José), who usurped the royal harem and eventually was quartered just like the Torres family itself.

The names of the characters have religious connotations. Both uncles of José—Manuel and Jesús—have names referring to Christ who is represented metaphorically in the Scriptures as a lamb; thus, the lamb José consumes recalls the sacrificed uncle Jesús (whom, like Saint Peter, he had denied) and the expulsion of Manuel, and thus symbolizes his guilt. Miriam, the name of his Moorish cousin, is reminiscent of another Spanish expulsion: that of the Jews in 1492.

José Torres, last male of the Spanish Torres family who had eluded all responsibility, admires his young Moorish cousin Yusuf (the Arab equivalent of José), a serious, responsible head of the family in Morocco. José is surprised to see his own features in a picture of Mohamed ben Yusuf ("son of Yusuf"), his host's great-grandfather who had restored the family in Fez to the position it once had in Spain. For some strange reason his body is not to be found in the Moorish cemetery known as "*Carnero*" which may be diversely translated as "Sheep" (perhaps echoing the lamb of the title), "Charnel House," or "Family Vault," all of which have implications related to José's memories. Maybe Yusuf's burial ground is in Spain, for here a decadent last scion of the Torres family, with common features, has betrayed his past and now asks: "What had happened to our family?"

José partially evades his growing sensations of guilt by attributing events to chance: his inexplicable visit to Fez instead of Marraquex where his business interests would have better been served, the surprise encounter with his Moorish "family," Gabrielillo's fate determined by lots, and the mere accident of finding himself in Republican or Nationalist territory during the war.

As Nelson Orringer points out, the central theme of "The Lamb's Head" is responsibility and evasion.[3] José had used his wits to extricate himself from difficult situations during the crisis, but had declined to do the same for his uncle Jesús or his associates. A clever impostor, he had assumed the roles of union leader, dependable Republican comrade, and finally a Nationalist. All the falseness of his conduct is brought to mind and relived in the day he spends in Fez with an outcast branch of his family, better forgotten, as he reverts to his former complacency after the symbolic expulsion of the lamb's head.

V   *"La vida por la opinión" ("One's Life for Reputation")*

Added to the second edition of *The Lamb's Head* in 1961, this story, written in 1955, marks the transition of Ayala's treatment of the Civil War from a serious to a more humorous vein combining both into tragicomedy. The narrator, distant from the war in time and space, hears refugees in America tell their stories, concluding that Spaniards tend to take politics too seriously. The war, he says, was a "bloody joke," particularly for the big powers who manipulated it, so that Spain was doomed from the start to Dante's admonition of hopelessness: *Lasciate ogni speranza* (Abandon all hope).

As a sort of prologue, he repeats the story of Andrés Manso, told to him by a teacher in exile. Inspired by the irony of Manso's name, meaning "gentle," or "tame," the victors of the war forced him into a bullring where he met his death. This sets the tone for the telling of stories with a twist of black humor. The narrator says that if it were a question of writing a story, he would choose another fugitive's account of his experiences and title it "One's Life for Reputation." The story concerns a secondary school teacher who worked in an institute created by the Republic. He remained hidden in a hollow place in his bedroom for nine years while his wife and mother claimed that he had disappeared. He entertained himself by editing an incomprehensible narrative composed of un-

usual words from the dictionary, and "without working, he had the
two things which man, according to the Archpriest, works
for—sustenance and a pleasurable woman."[4] In a moment of optimism at the end of World War II, the young couple abandon
themselves to "natural effusions, with no precautions or post-
cautions" (756), only to find out that their celebration had been
premature. As the volume of his absurd manuscript swells, so does
the belly of his careless wife, and due to a punctilious sense of
honor, he decides to leave his hiding place to assure that there will
be no public doubt as to the father of the baby. Through relatives,
he arranges to come to America to sell art objects so that he can
bring his mother, wife, and little daughter from Seville. The
narrator refers to Murillo's paintings of the Immaculate Conception, which leads to jokes about the baby's name, Concha, short for
Conception. The refugee offers the full name of "Unplanned
Conception" as he caresses his other creation—the absurd manuscript that has consumed the best years of his youth.

The title itself is a burlesque version of a quote from Calderón's
play *El alcalde de Zalamea (The Mayor of Zalamea).*[5] The point of
view is humorous, but the case of this poor man is just as atrocious
as that of Andrés Manso, for during nine years he is no more than a
mole, rat, or rabbit—animals to which he is compared. As if to
prove that "these are not stories" (as the narrator announces at the
beginning), the true story of Manuel Cortés Quero, former
Republican soldier and mayor, came to light in newspaper accounts
in 1969 when a general amnesty was declared in Spain and he
emerged from a house where he had hidden for thirty years!

Ayala refers to the title of his story as "classical" since its theme is
that exaggerated sense of honor which can be found in much of
Spain's classical theater, and particularly in that of Calderón. Only
in Spain would a man risk his life for his reputation, which, as our
author asserts in his essay "El punto de honor castellano" ("The
Castilian Point of Honor"), unjustly depends on the conduct of
another person: the woman for whom he is responsible.

VI *Unity in* The Lamb's Head

It should be recalled that Ayala, referring to the titles of stories in
The Usurpers, indicated that they were interchangeable. The same
is undoubtedly true of the carefully chosen brief titles of this

volume. The theme of "The Tagus," the incision of the Civil War into the heart of Spain, is applicable to all the stories. "The Message," of the first tale, assumes other forms in the well-intentioned message Santolalla brings to the mother of his victim ("The Tagus"), in the strange manuscript of the exiled teacher in "One's Life for Reputation," and in the messages transmitted subconsciously by memories of the past in almost all the stories. The title of "The Return" is applicable to what is literally accomplished in the form of a visit in "The Message" and "The Tagus," but also describes the return to the past via memories or its remnants as in "The Lamb's Head." The latter, which provides a fitting title for the whole volume, symbolizes all the victims and has religious overtones since the lamb as a reference to Jesus is suggested by numerous characters who are named for Christ: Manuel and Jesús in "The Lamb's Head," María Jesús and Manuel Abeledo in "The Return."

There are other common elements in the stories such as the presence of dogs which is even more pronounced in Ayala's later works. Severiano assumes a doglike expression of humiliation in "The Message," a dog named Chispa is a victim of violence in "The Tagus," and the narrator of "The Return" is pursued by dogs in a nightmare.

Two persistent motifs proceed from *The Usurpers:* the empty labyrinth and the impostors. When the narrator of "The Message" finally finds his way through the maze of detail presented by his cousin Severiano, he learns that "there was nothing in the desk, nothing in the side drawers, nothing in the compartments, absolutely nothing!" (632). The narrator of "The Return" comments: "I had done nothing; and that nothing was all for nothing" (704). The past of José Torres's family or families in "The Lamb's Head" seems like a labyrinth to him in which he comes face to face with himself and his conscience. There are many impostors who are compelled by weakness or circumstances to deceive others such as Abeledo in "The Return," Santolalla in "The Tagus," pretending to be a comrade of his victim, and Roque in "The Message," acting like a sophisticated world traveler.

A final theme is present in *The Lamb's Head:* the breakdown of effective verbal communication which marks the charged atmosphere of critical times, signified by undecipherable messages or manuscripts, profanity and the throwing of filth which displaces language ("The Tagus"), and uneasiness before unfamiliar speech ("The Lamb's Head").

In conclusion, the center of interest, as Ayala states in his proem, is civil war in the hearts of men, rather than upon the battlefield. For this reason he treats the actual state of combat in all the stories, except "The Tagus," in an oblique way to use the term offered by Keith Ellis—that is, by means of insinuation or memory.[6]

CHAPTER 6

Monkey Stories

IN 1955 Ayala published a book of six stories entitled *Historia de macacos (Monkey Story)*, also the title of the first selection. The overriding theme of these inventions is the human tendency to debase others by means of ridicule, practical jokes, gossip, or prejudice which can lead to tragic, pathetic, or even humorous consequences. It will be remembered that our author's interest in this type of human behavior stems from his first novel, *Tragicomedy of a Man Without a Spirit*, where Miguel Castillejo is the victim of a cruel trick. There is a scene in this novel in which Miguel, contemplating his image in a mirror, decides he resembles a simian, exclaiming: "A simian! But a simian in European dress; a circus monkey" (244).[1] Now in these stories which all qualify for the title of "Monkey Story," the tone is festive rather than serious, and Ayala achieves the most effective satire of the weaknesses of *homo ridiculus*.

I "*Historia de macacos*" ("*Monkey Story*")

In his essay *Razón del mundo (The World Explained)*, Ayala cites the need in the human species to program its existence and to aspire to a realization of its aims, for "conditions under which one cannot order his own conduct beyond elemental or immediate reactions will end up reducing his existence to an infra-human level."[2] This statement describes precisely the situation presented in "Monkey Story" where in the absence of meaningful purpose a tremendous state of boredom gives rise to the most absurd projects.

The narrator first tells how all the men in the small African colony enjoyed the favors of Rosa, "wife" of Robert, the Director of Expeditions and Shipping, who was seemingly ignorant of her amorous activities. He then describes the "bomb" which explodes when Robert announces at his farewell banquet, which he himself prepares to celebrate his imminent return to England, that the lady is really a prostitute who had joined him in a business venture, and a very profitable one, thanks to the generosity of those who benefitted by her friendship. The guests, all of them males, realize that the joke was on them and not on Robert. The administrator, Abarca, directs an insult to Rosa who replies triumphantly with an obscene gesture. The narrator, who insists on his unimportance, tries to find out if the natives are aware of these events, and consults Martín, the oldest European in the colony, a sort of retired tropical *conquistador* who has fathered many children among the natives. The old man indicates that the natives do know what has happened and adds an enigmatic comment about Robert: "Poor man."

To alleviate the tedium following the departure of the infamous pair, Abarca wagers that he is capable of eating a roasted monkey, for it is rumored that the natives do it as a ritualistic enactment of cannibalism. The enigmatic Martín again offers a mysterious prophecy: that there will be a wedding. Abarca wins the bet, in spite of general disappointment because he eats the monkey in a more palatable form: cut up with vegetables. With his winnings, he leaves for England to seek Rosa and marry her. He returns with the news that Rosa and Robert have married, sarcastically proclaiming his satisfaction that the latter has done an honorable act by endorsing, albeit *a posteriori*, the horns that had been put on him in the colony.

It is obvious that there are several monkeys in the story and that most of them are of the human variety, for like monkeys, humans imitate foolish actions and form a laughable spectacle—what the narrator calls "absurd comedy," farce, and pantomime. The Europeans put on a great show for the natives, who seem paradoxically more civilized and sophisticated than they are. This reversal is emphasized by the use of ironic hyperbole, for these poor souls, who for one reason or another find themselves isolated in this faraway colony with its muddy streets and shacks, try to imitate the life of the great capitals, designating their miserable surroundings with names like Imperial Avenue, the Great Plaza, the Government Palace, and the Country Club. The narrator refers to the governor as "the Omnipotent," and speaks of the activities in the colony as their "African campaign." The farewell banquet becomes a great "social event" and something as ridiculous as Abarca's bet elicits debates, the formation of political parties, newspaper articles, and radio broadcasts as the "big public issue" of the moment. As a sort of comedy within a comedy, the scene of Abarca's monkey feast is enacted before an "illustrious senate," a term taken from Golden Age Theater, referring to the nobles present in the audience, and another theatrical expression, *"hacer mutis"* (to exit from the stage), is used.

Ayala effectively employs a technique which the Spanish Golden Age playwright, Lope de Vega, made both famous and popular: lying with the truth. At the beginning of the farewell banquet, when Abarca and Robert discuss which of them is more indebted to the other, it sounds like mere courtesy, but it turns out that Robert indeed owes a debt of thanks to Rosa's clients. Martín's enigmatic announcement of a coming wedding seems absurd, but to everyone's surprise it is a true statement which refers to Robert's wedding, not Abarca's. It would seem to be a lie when Rosa confides to the narrator that she is unhappy with her "husband's" coldness toward her, but, as later events prove, she did care for him and was concerned with his indifference. "She didn't give the impression of lying" (785), says the narrator, and essentially she wasn't.

It is the narrator, in fact, who reveals to us the human side of the much maligned Rosa, a perspective made possible by his neutral condition. While his former wife had placed him in the maximum situation of ridicule as a cuckold, Rosa had treated him with kindness and understanding upon realizing his impotence, which the narrator blames on nerves and the tropics. It is interesting to see how well he assesses collective events but, at the same time, he cannot perceive the truth of his own weakness. His principal concern is to avoid becoming a monkey but he is also worried that the colonial functionaries may be laughed at by the natives. The cast of characters is certainly open to ridicule: the clownish Bruno Salvador, the homosexual radio announcer Toñito Azucena (whose last name, meaning "lily," says all), and the bovine Smith Matías.

The narrator insists that the mysterious Martín is in "limbo," but it is he and his colleagues who really are there. When the monkey is eaten by Abarca, the other half of the animal is carried to Martín, who is found lying dead on the kitchen floor, having died during the siesta. The old patriarch and seer has been dislodged from his "eternal hammock," and it now appears to be Abarca's turn to assume the same posture, lying drunk on the divan in the club as if to take the place of the other, since he too has eaten monkey meat. Having completed his only project, avenging Robert's trick, he can now retreat to limbo.

As we have seen in Ayala's other fictions, there are several people "bewitched," first by Rosa, a sort of queen who maintains order and expectation among the "monkeys," and second, by Abarca, in his exhibition of sublimated cannibalism.

II   *"La barba del capitán" ("The Captain's Beard")*

A woman about to be married narrates an incident remembered from her childhood involving Captain Ramírez, a subordinate of her father's whose dignity seemed to be represented by his beard. The Captain was drinking one day in headquarters and allowed his beard to be shaved off so that when his wife awoke the next morning, she didn't recognize the man alongside her as her husband, and raised a commotion which caused the neighbors to break in. The female narrator feels ashamed when she imagines Captain Ramírez, minus beard and clothes, subjected to public ridicule. She asks herself why she recalls now that absurd episode which at the time evoked feelings which tortured her tender heart and made her eyes, "just opened to life," shed tears. She remembers her indignation at her father's delight in mortifying his embarrassed subordinate and asks what evil deep within the human heart makes even someone as kind as her father take pleasure in ridiculing someone else. The story is repeated by others, but the version offered by the military chaplain causes her to envision the naked pair as the Adam and Eve of her Bible illustrations. The narrator wonders why the episode lingers in her memory, a question the reader is, by inference, invited to answer.

Ellis comments that "in none of Ayala's stories do we find a protagonist as highly sensitive as the narrator of 'The Captain's Beard.' "[3] The story proves that comedy or tragedy is essentially in the eyes of the beholder, for what was a vaudeville incident for others awakened her compassion and sadness, and even years later inspires soul-searching and suffering in her. The tone of nostalgic sadness of this story anticipates Ayala's later creations of "Días felices" ("Happy Days").

"The Captain's Beard" is another "monkey story" because the captain is the victim of a joke which makes others laugh at him. The narrator is the only person who seems to comprehend that human frailty—the captain's ingenuousness and an afternoon of drinking—made him vulnerable to ridicule in what she sees as a dehumanizing military atmosphere. Now she herself embarks on marriage, forming her own combination of Adam and Eve. If before, as a child and an outsider, she had not been able to express her concern for a vulnerable human being, now she must face life responsibly, a perspective which in itself brings the sadness of expulsion from the Garden of Eden.

III *"Encuentro" ("Meeting")*

A minimum of linguistic suggestion with dialogue punctuated by French and Italian expressions, colloquialisms, and nicknames, locates this story specifically in Buenos Aires. Additional local color is contributed by references to famous tangos encrusted in the narrative. These tangos, identified by Rosario Hiriart as "Golden Age," "My Beautiful Julián," "Grand Victoria Hotel," "The Professor," evoke a melodramatic world of nostalgia, sentimentality, and unfulfilled dreams which is the essence of the tango.[4]

The meeting suggested by the title is that of Vatteone, alias "Boneca," with a skinny and weary woman whom he runs into and recognizes as his old flame Nelly, alias "Filly," "Nelly Bicycle" (ridden by many), and "Chajá" (like this Argentine bird, she wore feathers over her skinny body). The story follows their conversation and inner thoughts which reveal their relationship in the past. Nelly had been very popular and was the girl friend of Saldanha, a rich old Brazilian, while Vatteone, jealous and humiliated by being her errand boy, had suffered in silence. Now Vatteone is proud and satisfied to see himself wealthy and successful in politics while his once sought-after Nelly shows the devastating effects of age. At the same time, Nelly finds him fat and swollen: not at all an impressive spectacle. She has since married Muñoz, who had defended her before others; Vatteone has married Beba, "fat, white and pompous." Bored by Vatteone's conversation about politics and his success as an opportunist under Perón, Nelly flees from his bravado to return home to her husband now ill and confined to his wicker chair. Enjoining her to come to him if she needs anything, Vatteone adjusts his tie before a store window with enormous self-satisfaction.

As we have noted, the sentimentality and nostalgia of the story is accentuated by allusions to tangos, but the theme is also reminiscent of verses of the nineteenth-century poet Campoamor treating the subject of the ravages of time in very commonplace contexts. Vatteone's exclamation on seeing Nelly: "God! This thing here . . ." (810), recalls Campoamor's poem "Las cosas del tiempo" ("Things Time Does") in which a man and woman who have not seen each other for many years ask themselves respectively: "My God. And is this he? . . . My God. And is this she?" In another Campoamor poem called "Los dos espejos" ("The Two Mirrors"), a man, forty years old like Vatteone, having lost youth, love, and faith, sees himself as old and ugly both physically and spiritually. As opposed to Ayala's character, who is too arrogant to recognize any flaws in himself, this man can. The theme of Ayala's story is time and its effects not only on the body but also on the soul. Vatteone, delighted with his own image, scorns Nelly, but it is obvious to the reader that he is perhaps morally worse than she. He is married to a woman he can't stand, although he sports his material wealth and is so rich that he does not count the change from the large bill he uses to pay for his treat.

Nelly, who regarded him before as a *petit farceur*—a small buffoon, but a nice fellow—sees that Vatteone has changed. The reader easily perceives that he has simply turned into a *grand farceur* instead of the small one he was before. Ironically, Nelly had really liked him more than her wealthy Brazilian lover who Vatteone now imitates. She never could stand Saldanha's "airs of condescending superiority" and was bored by his conversation, exactly as she is now bored by the same things in Vatteone. Vatteone, on the other hand, assumes that she is impressed by his money, but we observe that she has never been addicted to riches. As Vatteone recalls, she preferred making love to having furs, and ended up marrying for love. So by emulating his old rival, he has become a bigger "monkey" than ever.

Vatteone's thoughts exemplify the human tendency to belittle others in order to raise one's own ego, but we see that these are efforts to protect oneself from the passage of time which eventually humbles even the most inflated ego. The inexorable changes wrought by time are not only physical, but also psychological, for Muñoz's silence and quiescence, which delighted Nelly years ago, are now only irritating traits to her. Time as a presiding force in the story is further accentuated by explicit references to clocks and time. Vatteone recalls his impatience, watching the café clock when he anxiously awaited Nelly's arrival. Nelly looks at her watch, wondering if her husband is doing the same, and as she gets up to leave, she tells Vatteone that she has no more time, and rushes home to her waiting husband.

IV *"The Last Supper"*

"The Last Supper," whose title is given directly in English, begins with a "providential" meeting which takes place in the ladies' room of a New York restaurant when Trude invades the privacy of a woman whom she recognizes as her former schoolmate from "the Old World," Sara Gross. The two friends tell their stories over cokes. Sara had come to America soon after her marriage. Trude arrived that very morning from Argentina with her husband who is marketing an infallible rat poison under the brand name "The Last Supper." This name, explains Trude, was inspired by the bombing of Milan when Da Vinci's famous painting was thought lost, and was devised by Bruno (an "exquisite spirit" and "true artist"), as a sort of artistic compensation. She tells Sara how Bruno came across the formula during the years he spent in a German concentration camp. Without going into details, she mentions that she was made to run along the Central Boulevard on all fours with a muzzle, and alludes to the unspeakable infamy to which her son was subjected (not explicitly described). At that moment Sara observes with alarm that her friend "opened her mouth wide just like a dog and broke out in tears, hiccups and sobs, almost barking" (826). Sara manages to console her, assuring her that it's all over now, and Trude recovers her composure, switching again to her former enthusiasm about the future of her husband's marvelous product in America.

This is one of Ayala's most powerful stories, growing in intensity from the almost compulsive chatter of its opening paragraphs into a shattering scene of anguish in which the reader, like Sara Gross, listens attentively with growing alarm. The theme of human degradation is suggested immediately in the introductory setting of a public toilet where Sara is "enthroned." As Ayala expresses in his book of essays *El problema del liberalismo (The Problem of Liberalism)*, man, deprived of freedom, is degraded to an animal condition.[5] The trauma to which Trude was subjected, reducing her to a dog's conduct, has left permanent lesions. Of even greater consequence, degradation fosters further degradation as we can see in Bruno's case where it has international repercussions. As Trude reports, the rat poison, marketed under such an attractive name, became so popular in South America that it was widely used for suicides. The fact that a person described as refined and artistic is reduced to the act of creating a poison later ingested by humans for suicidal purposes is repulsive, and is even more so when it involves the commercial degradation of a religious motif. Packaged in round boxes on which the painting is reproduced in color, the product, in light of the opening scene of the story, evokes a vision of toilet paper. The desire to forget bad memories and think of the future is not so easily attained, for the effects of man's bestiality toward his fellow man are not readily exterminated. Even when it is packaged artistically and given fancy names, poison is still poison.

V *"Un cuento de Maupassant"* (*"A Story by Maupassant"*)

This story, one of Ayala's least studied works, begins with what appears to be a lecture about plots which "belong" to certain writers who are known for their "reiterated rendering of a certain type of human experience" (827), but there is a hint of facetiousness as the speaker adds that these plots may even be in the writers' lost works. From the initial high level of literary theory, there is some descent as the speaker's pipe and beer appear and it becomes obvious that he is speaking informally to a group of young intellectuals among whom the narrator is situated. His role in the story is very brief, informing us at this point that the speaker is an "illustrious writer" and that the character about whom the story revolves, Antuña, is a well-known philosopher. The lecture then is only a prelude to an anecdote about the oracular intellectual Antuña, an "exceptional man" who is universally respected, although he has neither written nor expressed his profound and hermetic ideas. The "illustrious author" insinuates that these ideas are in fact those of Antuña's wife Xantipa, a name which immediately establishes the poor man's resemblance to Socrates who also did not commit his ideas to paper and was continually martyred by his irascible wife Xantipa. The speaker's story, which he identifies as a plot of Maupassant, explains how Antuña was alienated from his generous friend Durán due to a dispute between their wives. It seems that Durán's wife had given Antuña's wife a dress which her seamstress had inadvertently made the same as her own, and when both women appeared wearing the same dress, Xantipa demanded a public apology. The speaker, a friend of Antuña's, tried to intervene, invoking the literary tradition of Shakespeare's "Taming of the Shrew" and Juan Manuel's medieval story of "The Young Man

Who Married an Ill-tempered Wife," but Antuña reminds him of his wife's formidable biceps.

Ayala's story is really quite complex. It is at the same time a spoof on intellectuals like Antuña and the "illustrious writer," and a fictional examination of the literary problem of originality and imitation. The intellectuals are less than admirable. Antuña is enigmatic, silent, and ambiguous, qualities which have won him a reputation as a brilliant philosopher. The writer purports to edify his youthful audience so they will not waste their talents as Antuña has done, but his motives become suspect as we see him gossip about the private life of his "friend." The envy he attributes to Xantipa for "airing" her husband's dirty clothes in public is probably his own in publicizing the unfortunate incident and approaching the philosopher's neighbors in search of "Antuña stories."

There are numerous literary allusions and analogies in the story which focus upon the problem of originality in literature. The "illustrious writer" calls his anecdote a story by Maupassant and mentions his experience of writing a fiction which "belonged" to Henry James. At the end, when the narrator reappears among the listeners, another young man remarks that though the lecturer's plot may be taken from Maupassant, the main character is from Dostoevski. It is, of course, ludicrous to compare Antuña to a tortured, suffering Dostoevskian hero.

The title Ayala chooses for his story has never been analyzed with regard to how the fiction achieves a unique combination of form and content identifiable as a Maupassant work. According to A. H. Wallace, the story "*Une Famille*" ("A Family") typifies a number of this famous nineteenth-century French novelist's stories which show how marriage destroys friendships between old male cronies and express the author's "repugnance at how the wife is always certain to drag her husband down to her level."[6] While many of Maupassant's stories show admiration for women for not accepting marriage as a form of servitude, the male usually deludes himself that he is the master while the woman gains ascendancy over him. Maupassant condemns the weakness of man and regards marriage as an imposition. Perhaps Ayala's "illustrious writer" would have pleased Maupassant, for "among the strangely few men who enjoyed Maupassant's unstinting admiration, most had chosen celibacy and so were relatively safe from acts of weakness that so often characterize a husband's behavior and which would have lowered them in his esteem."[7] In the French writer's story "In the Spring," we find the following warnings: "In love, monsieur, men are the artists, and women are the dealers"[8] and "beware of love. It is more dangerous than brandy, bronchitis or pleurisy! It never forgives and makes everybody commit irreparable follies."[9]

There is an extension of the Maupassant analogy in the lecturer's allusion to one of his own creations which produced a Henry James work since James admired Maupassant and translated his works into English. James's stories often treat the theme of art and artists, and in "The Lesson of the Master," 1888, a "great novelist" expresses the opinion that marriage is incompatible with writing, perhaps a rationalization for James's never having married. The story treats the deleterious effect of marriage on a writer's aims and image which is precisely the theme of the Antuña story offered by Ayala's lecturer.

The literary issue of originality and imitation is posed in dual form: first it is developed on the artistic level where allusions to Shakespeare, Juan Manuel, James, and Maupassant demonstrate that total originality of plot is virtually impossible. The literary problem is parodied on the everyday level by the indignation of the two women wearing the same dresses. A suitable comment is provided by Ayala in his essay *The World Explained* with regard to the fear of plagiarism: "Many cases of plagiarism cause explosions of hysterics, even more comical if one takes into account the scant spiritual importance of the property under dispute."[10] The knowing smile the "illustrious writer" directs to his audience may indicate a parable in his Antuña story.

VI *"El colega desconocido"* ("The Unknown Colleague")

The narrator, who is a writer, relates an unnerving experience which befell his "mature, fat and famous" friend Pepe Orozco, the toast of the best literary circles. Invited to an embassy party, he had met Alberto Stéfani, also a writer, whose ignorance of his work deeply wounded Orozco's pride. Wondering how Stéfani had been invited by no less a personage than the Minister of Education, Orozco investigates the works of this unknown colleague and discovers to his dismay that the "mediocre" books of Stéfani, the reputed "philosopher of the heart," are repeatedly published in copious editions while his own fame is limited to a much smaller group of admirers. Orozco's descent into a literary "underworld" whose existence he had never suspected outside of the "legitimate order of letters" brings him to the realization that it is his own group which inhabits an underworld and that he has been guilty of an error of perspective based more on scorn than ignorance.

After the discovery, Orozco attends a family party where another "apparition from the other literary world" (850) is treated as a celebrity while he is unknown, even among his own family, as an artist. He comes to the conclusion that he had ventured into an inferno without a guide, unlike Dante who had his Virgil, and consoles himself that "in art, merit is not judged by popularity, but by the intrinsic value of one's works" (851). The narrator, unconvinced by the value of the test of time, asks his friend why they as writers insist on publishing and seeking the approval of their contemporaries. Orozco calls it a human weakness, but the narrator considers being read essential to creation. Orozco says he writes for God; the other states that he writes to be read by mortal and fallible men; finally the famous writer concedes to the narrator: "As for you, it must be that you write for the love of God so that his creatures may read your work. For men, yes, but for the love of God: an act of charity you practice unceasingly and indefatigably" (853).

In "The Unknown Colleague," Ayala treats fictionally a problem examined in a number of his essays: the writer's purpose and his public. Leaving the identification of the narrator with the author of the story as a moot point (Angel del Río sees them as one and the same, Keith Ellis does not), the piece may be considered as an examination of conscience developed via two alter egos. Official approval, literary prizes, and the tastes of the masses, leaning toward sentimental vulgarity, are enough to cause a serious loss of self-confidence in an author of conscience which can only be restored by a strong vocation and faith. It is to Ayala's credit that he considers a question which many in the fine arts refrain from discussing: the relative unpopularity of "good literature," for the fact that the contemporary writer who has sold most books in the Spanish language (millions!) is Corín Tellado, a prolific author of sentimental novels, is something to be pondered by serious writers. Orozco learns not to scorn what for a great many people is "culture" and that one cannot overlook the public and write exclusively "for the love of God." The ideal is evidently to be aware of the great reading public of the "underworld" and to hope to turn it someday into the "upperworld."

CHAPTER 7

Longer Novels

IN 1958 Ayala's novel *Muertes de perro (Dog's Death)* was published, followed four years later by another, *El fondo del vaso (The Bottom of the Glass)*, but as a significant indication of their harmonious relationship, they were originally intended to be joined, with the author's approval, in one volume in the Italian translation. *The Bottom of the Glass* may be considered a sequel because it is set in the same country as *Dog's Death* shortly after the events therein described. Ayala further emphasizes the relationship between the two novels by having the protagonist of the sequel comment upon the narration of the previous work, much in the same fashion that Don Quijote, in the second part of Cervantes's great novel, discusses the first part.

I Dog's Death

Confined to his wheelchair, the narrator Pinedito reconstructs by means of letters, reports, documents, conversations, and memoirs, the saga of a tropical Latin American republic under the rule of the tyrant Bocanegra. The latter has been killed by his private secretary Tadeo Requena, said to be his illegitimate son, who in turn was eliminated by Cortina, who fell down the palace steps and was supplanted by Olóriz who now wields the power. The cast of characters is thus presented as a vertiginous enumeration of victims and their respective rise and fall.

Using principally the memoirs of Tadeo Requena as his source, Pinedo reconstructs what could be called exemplary episodes illustrating the degenerative effects of Bocanegra's reign on individuals and institutions. One incident describes public consternation when, during the solemn rendering of the national Hymn—which, "like the country's history," has no beginning or end in its single motif—a dog barks along with the anthem while the taciturn and distracted dictator neglects to give the sign to end the hymn. Another farce indicative of the times occurs in the reception offered the President in the National Academy of Fine Arts and Letters which Pinedo calls an "orgy of bestiality and humiliation." Still another takes place in the "interlude of the stolen Christ Child;" here the "celestial lyricist" Carmelo Zapata feels obligated to protect public morality by kidnapping a figurine of popular art from an exhibit because it shows "exaggerated virility in a figure of tender age, probably due to a knot in the wood" (913).[1] Another episode points out the danger of being a foreigner, specifically a Spanish immigrant, when Camarasa publishes an article construed to poke fun at the "purest patriotic sentiments" of his host country, and is subsequently eliminated—partly due to the anonymous diatribe Pinedo publishes against him. Servile (canine) behavior appears when the American ambassador, Mr. Grogg, presents a dog named Fanny to the First Lady as a substitute for her pet that died—an example of "intervention of the great powers" (931). Tadeo Requena, brought from obscurity to the palace to become the trusted "guard dog" of Bocanegra, hangs the dog which his tutor Luisito Rosales had taught to bark the National Hymn as a birthday gift for the President. The hapless tutor had pinned his hopes for moral vindication regarding his prowess as an educator upon the dog's performance. An atmosphere of adulation and bestiality has led to the disappearance of the last human sentiment in a general degradation which even the intellectual Pinedito feels he cannot curb. As Ayala has repeatedly stated, the thrust of his novel is not intended to be taken as political or even social, but rather moral: as a portrait of a world without values (our present world) in which the only road to salvation lies in scrutinizing the depths of one's own conscience.[2]

Some critics (Hugo Rodríguez-Alcalá, José Marra López) feel that Ayala has excluded from his novel all noble sentiments, but certainly the fact that even the most repugnant characters receive their just desserts either by the hand of others or before the tribunal of their own conscience would vitiate this criticism, for the latter is indeed an act of human dignity. There are in addition other characters, like Senator Lucas Rosales, brutally assassinated, and his wife, living in the United States, who exhibit noble traits.

Pinedito, the crippled narrator of *Dog's Death*, is very conscious of his literary and historical mission and considers himself privi-

leged to be in a position of marginality from which he can observe
events objectively. He criticizes Tadeo Requena's literary pretensions and egocentricity (unjust considerations in dealing with one's
memoirs) as well as his anachronistic use of later data to illuminate
past occurrences retrospectively (exactly as Pinedo does himself).
The reader can see that Pinedo is guilty of the same weaknesses—in
writing and in action—of which he accuses others, rolling to the
bottom of the abyss in his wheelchair, as it were, by killing the
usurper Olóriz when he had considered himself superior to the
events which took place around him.

In *The World Explained,* Ayala treats in essay form the problem
of the intellectual who wants to maintain his independence within a
society in a state of crisis but finds himself "paralysed by it" with
his own conscience contaminated by the crisis.[3] Pinedo provides a
graphic example of this phenomenon, symbolically by his physical
paralysis, and morally, by following in suit the abjectness he
deplores in Tadeo Requena by assassinating a political chief. We are
aware that Requena and Pinedo have much in common, being
clandestine writers and cold, sarcastic types, and that only Pinedo's
paralysis detains him from becoming another Requena until the
end. Thus, the intellectual who thought himself a mere spectator is
caught in the web, deluding himself that he has "risen" from
chronicler to a "national hero, meritorious citizen to whom the
grateful Nation should erect a statue" (1017).

A multiplicity of "I's" in various first-person narrations enables
us to approach the characters' inner thoughts by establishing an intimacy between themselves and the readers, and by making us feel
involved to the extent that we listen to their confessions and react
with compassion, surprise, or indignation. We too feel guilty
because "one never knows, one never knows anything, about
himself or others" (1012). The tutor's poor daughter María Elena
asks herself why she submitted to Tadeo while her father's body lay
in the next room, and Requena perceives some obscure image
reflected in her idiot brother Angelo as he too has his moment of
"touching bottom" within his conscience. Ayala's aim is to involve
us in these critical confessions of his characters, and this is one of
the reasons why *Dog's Death* is so different from Miguel Angel
Asturias's *Señor Presidente (Mr. President)* and Ramón del Valle-
Inclán's *Tirano Banderas (Tyrant Banderas),* which, though they
treat the similar dictator theme, employ techniques designed to
keep the reader at a distance and to impress him as spectacle.

Stylistically, our author communicates the degradation rampant in Bocanegra's domain by means of several devices. First, the title symbolizes the bestiality, servility, and sad fate of many characters. Pinedo points out the constant presence of dogs in comic and dramatic roles. The human counterparts are easy to identify: trained dogs like the tutor Luisito Rosales; faithful dogs which suddenly turn on their owners like Tadeo Requena; hungry, devouring animals like Bocanegra; and the female, Doña Concha, the First Lady.

Another way in which Ayala suggests the pernicious influence of the tyrant is by allusions to the animalistic aspects of man, that is to say, his natural functions, which, as María Elena realizes, work against the spirit. Our first view of Bocanegra takes place in his bathroom, "sanctuary whose access implied the supreme honor of the state" (871), where he is posed on his filthy throne. Pinedo's insignificance consists of being able to observe people from behind, observing the "seat of their pants," as he says. There are risqué puns on the word *"fondo"* ("bottom") when Pinedo's aunt, the informant Loreto (whose name suggests *loro,* parrot), affirms that Bocanegra's only interest is the "bottom of the glass and other bottoms." Pinedo understands this remark only too well as an allusion to the dictator's vices, but pretends to interpret it as a reference to "funds," another meaning of the word *fondos.* The name of Doña Concha's dog (Fanny) and the nickname of Bocanegra, "P. P.," play upon English colloquialisms. Concha is colloquially a term designating the female sexual organ, and the name Bocanegra ("Blackmouth") suggests a filthy orifice, while that of Olóriz, the usurper, insinuates foul odor *(olor).*

Another effective technique is the application of Latin terms and religious vocabulary in erotic contexts, indicating the prostitution of everything noble as a corollary of the curtailment of freedom. Doña Concha (a nickname for *Concepción,* meaning Conception) ends her days after having been raped by "thousands of prisoners" in the "pigsty" Prison of the Immaculate Conception. She is referred to as the *"Gran Mandona"* which means "Big Boss" but which is obviously a deliberate alteration of Madonna. Tadeo's carnal relations with the wife of his benefactor Bocanegra are consistently described by Latin and religious allusions. Requena recognizes that he is no Biblical "chaste Joseph" and he hears Doña Concha's "confessions" to gain information. At a sign of *sursum corda,* used to order a religious congregation to rise, Tadeo rises to her bidding. St. John's term *consummatum est,* repeated by Jesus in the Gospels, marks the culmination of Concha's and Tadeo's relations, and the Pope's blessing to Rome and the world, *urbe et orbi,* describes the universal admiration of the First Lady's pectoral attractions. The parody is not to be construed as demeaning to the church, but rather as a device for showing the depths to which these people have fallen. The spirit of Luisito Rosales, Tadeo's tutor who appears at a séance, explains his similar use of Greek after calling the medium *coprófaga* (eater of filth) as a means of permitting "cultured people to form certain concepts, eluding the vulgar locutions of the common people" (995).

As Rosario Hiriart indicates, literary allusions also produce parody since Tadeo's similarity to Calderón's character Segismundo from *La vida es sueño (Life Is a Dream)* or to Tirso de Molina's classical *Vergonzoso en palacio (Shy Fellow at the Palace)* is hardly exact except for the fact that they all are brought to the court.

In all these techniques used by Ayala, it is difficult to determine their degree of comedy, for we find ourselves entertained by them even when they accompany less than funny situations. Pinedo recognizes this effect when he comments that "frivolity can reach tragic dimensions" (927) and "if it weren't for the tragic consequences to which all this has led us, it would be funny" (994).

Part of the ambiguity of this humor stems from Ayala's dense and pervading irony which has not been fully appreciated, particularly with regard to the novel's setting. Keith Ellis claims that Spanish American dictatorships are presented,[4] and José Blanco Amor calls it an American novel.[5] Recalling the subtle transplanting of time setting in *The Usurpers* where present-day concerns are projected into the past, it is plausible to consider the possibility of a similar transference of place setting in *Dog's Death.* Dictatorships are not exclusive to Spanish America, where, in fact, they have been explained as an outgrowth of the conquistador from Spain. The humorous reports of the Spanish minister to his office in Madrid, lamenting "the barbarous social atmosphere of this American land," are flagrantly ironical in view of the atmosphere in Spain itself at this time. It is not farfetched to see a similarity between P. P. Bocanegra (for *Padre de los Pelados,* or Patron of the Poor) and F. F. Bahamonde (Francisco Franco Bahamonde) in the double initials and the composite names beginning with "B" formed by the same number of letters and syllables.

The episodical nature of *Dog's Death* reveals Ayala's experience in short narrative, but at the same time, the expert manner in which these episodes are structured is the work of a master novelist. In a really fine study, Monique Joly describes the structure of the novel as a system of perspectives.[6] She notices that in the first ten chapters no less than eleven characters and their deaths are mentioned so that the plan is a puzzle in inverse order (Z to A) as the circumstances of their disappearance are revealed. This systematic anticipation demands collaboration on the part of the reader who is required to readjust his concepts as new versions are offered. Ms. Joly discusses the various versions of certain incidents which differ enormously in point of view and in the tone with which they are recounted.

If these procedures seem confusing and vertiginous to the reader, the events so presented are no less so to the characters. The multiple, changing realities cause several characters to experience dizziness and nausea, reflecting the uncertainty of their environment. Conflicting reports, conversations, and memoirs show that historical events cannot be accurately given by only one point of view nor can they be reliably communicated by a supposedly objective observer as true objectivity is impossible. While Ayala's disruption of time sequence represents clever artistic manipulation, it also parallels the manner in which the past generally serves us in the present. Recall is triggered at random and does not necessarily reflect the actual order in which events occurred.

Another comment on these structural techniques is provided by none other than José Lino Ruiz, the protagonist of *The Bottom of the Glass*, who sees the reappearance of certain episodes as Pinedo's stratagem to slant the novel: "The catalogue of atrocities that Pinedo selects is minimal in spite of the agglomerated way he presents them, for which reason there is no real basis for the truculent impression that nevertheless is transmitted effectively" (1031). In view of the fact that both the critic (José Lino) and the object of his criticism (Pinedito) are Ayala's creations, our author's explanation of the novel's structure and his defense against anticipated accusations of excessive cruelty are cleverly veiled in the fiction itself.

II The Bottom of the Glass

It is obvious that times have changed in the same Spanish American country of *Dog's Death*, now freed from tyrants and enjoying prosperity, jobs, and industrial growth. The moral climate, however, has not changed, for the oppressive power of government has simply been replaced by that of money. The patriotic and civic exhibitions favored by Bocanegra have yielded to pageants of nude beauties patronized by commercial potentates, while youthful street gangs and offbeat religious cults attract other sectors of the population.

Whereas Pinedito tries to imagine a glorious future free from the domination of Bocanegra, José Lino Ruiz, successful businessman and narrator of *The Bottom of the Glass*, views the "unforgettable President" as a hero and patriot who represents the glorious days of law and order, and aspires to vindicate his memory by writing a book. This ambitious project, for which he has solicited the collaboration of the Spaniard José Rodríguez, an experienced newspaperman, is never fulfilled. The two disagree and Lino's manuscript then becomes his own personal vindication. He recounts, with an attitude of complacent superiority, how he had disappeared to the "nether world" (Mexico) during the days of terror following Bocanegra's assassination, accompanied by Candy, a poor country *mestiza* whom he had employed and turned into his attractive lover in much the same way that Bocanegra had sponsored Tadeo Requena's transformation into his polished personal secretary. Candy now favors young Luisito Rodríguez, the son of his ex-collaborator, and Lino's dubious friend Doménech intercedes by procuring her a job in his bank (which, of course, displeases Lino) and by convincing her to break with Jr. Rodríguez, whose dead, beaten body is later found not far from Candy's house.

The second part of the novel is composed of news reports from *The Commerce*, describing Lino's implication in the murder, his preventive arrest, and subsequent bankruptcy. The newspaper exploits the "sordid relations" between him and Candy, and reluctantly prints the rival paper's account of Jr. Rodríguez's involvement in a street gang whose rivalry with others and assault on a cult temple (as far as the reader can see) probably had something to do with the crime. In this satirical newspaper whodunit, it is obvious that the news media, purportedly committed to objectivity and impartiality, supplies conjecture in the absence of facts and excuses the transgressions of sons of distinguished members of society as harmless mischief.

The final section transcribes Lino's thoughts during his imprisonment in the Miserere Jail. Shocked by his wife's pathetic confession of having deceived him with his ex-collaborator Luis Rodríguez, his first reaction is to blame her for all the complications resulting from his involvement with the Rodríguez family and Candy, but finally he comes to realize that he alone bears the blame for all that has happened to him and for his wife's infidelity.

Intentional word play throughout the novel is used to insinuate the continuing decay of values in an environment dominated by disintegrating social relationships. The title is an echo of Loreto's assertion in *Dog's Death* that Bocanegra was interested only in the "bottom of the glass," for that is precisely where the sediment collects. The idiomatic meaning of the expression *"en el fondo"* may be translated as "basically" or "essentially," suggesting that the moral climate of the country in Lino's era has not really changed. At the end, Lino "touches bottom" in the examination of his own conscience, encountering there the sediment of guilt which had collected there for many years.

Ayala particularly enjoys altering proper names to solicit from the reader certain attitudes toward his characters. The old lecher Cipriano Medrano, czar of the liquor industry, becomes familiarly Don Ano-Ano (meaning "anus"), for like the unforgettable Bocanegra (also suggestive of anus), he is the object of public veneration. Lino dreams about Medrano, and in his nightmare, the brand called Vermouth of the Isle of *Capri* (in itself a symbol of voluptuousness) changes to *Cipri,* pointing out Cipriano Medrano's egotism. In a *lapsus linguae* Medrano changes to Mengano and then Menguano (from *menguar,* to decay, while the name Mengano is used colloquially to mean "so-and-so") when Lino dreams that *"medró Mengano"* (so-and-so grew richer). The word play stresses the character's essential vulgarity and moral decay. The title of one of the beauty queens is Miss In-Co-Lo (for *Local Industry and Commerce*), but the last two syllables insinuate the same orifice parodied in the nickname Don Ano-Ano. Sexual anomalies are satirized by plays on names and words; for example, the name of one of the beauty contest judges—Alicia Albertona—is the feminization of the masculine name Alberto. The members of one of the street gangs are called *"doñas"* (women) until they commit sufficient acts of violence to merit the coveted title of *"Dueños"* (Bosses).

As in *Dog's Death,* religious and Biblical allusions serve ironically as a hint of the perversion of values. Lino views himself upon his return from Mexico as an "exultant Lazarus" risen from the dead.

Candelaria, whose name represents the Catholic feast of the Purification, is turned into the delectable "Candy." Lino refers to Rodríguez's wife as Our Lady of Capital Stupidity and to Pinedito as the *Ecce homo* of the wheelchair; but he himself becomes an example of *Ecce homo* in the jail, formerly a convent, appropriately named Miserere ("Have mercy," the opening words of the Fiftieth Psalm of the Vulgate) where he further suffers what he calls the "INRI" of his tearful Magdalena's confession of unfaithfulness. Lino likens his dreams in jail to those of Joseph the Chaste, to whom he can hardly be compared. The ironic nature of these religious allusions disappears at the end when he exclaims *mea culpa* (I am to blame) and implores God's help, not just for himself, but for all of us.

Literary references, a constant in Ayala's fiction, include Calderón, Shakespeare, Espronceda, Bretón de los Herreros, Zorrilla, and Garcilaso de la Vega. Rosario Hiriart, who discusses these allusions in her book on this theme, also notes that Corina is a suffering but unfaithful Penelope who weaves a complicated *linen (Lino)* in which her husband is caught up and undone, at least in his own assessment of his situation.

Classical myths are deliberately deflated by parody. Lino is an Orpheus in reverse because, according to Rodríguez, he entered Inferno to flee from his "beloved" Euridice, Corina. The description of the grotesque beauty contest, which anticipates the future ravages of time, refers to Paris's famous selection of Venus, and the idiot girl whose seduction by Jr. Rodríguez's gang leads to their assault on Happy God's Temple, is called a Helen of Troy. The cuckold Lino finally sees himself as a horned Minotaur imprisoned in a labyrinth.

The repeated use of governmental terminology represents the exaggerated importance Lino attributes to his individual interests while revealing at the same time his disdain toward the system. He regards himself as "the old oppressive metropolis" (1659) from which Candy dreams of liberating herself. As a merchant, Lino views her as his possession with "improvements made in the property." The beauty contest is ridiculed in terms of suffrage and plebiscite, and Don Ano-Ano is "czar of an alcoholic empire" ensconced in a "citadel," refusing to give up his throne or permit his children any "autonomy." Doménech's intervention in Lino's problem becomes a delicate "diplomatic mission" and Lino's fall is likened to that of Rome, Spain, and Britain.

Finally, it should be noted that the animal motif persists. The dogs of yesteryear are gone, replaced by a more democratic variety: the tadpole, toad, and water worm Pinedo; the parrot, nag, and cat Corina; the pig Rodríguez; the lamb, red ant, and "harmless dead mosquito" Candy; and Lino, self-characterized as a burro, rat, deer, lamb, and—most dreaded of all fauna among Spanish males—cornupete, complete with cage and bars.

José Lino Ruiz is one of Ayala's most poignant characters. The first-person narrative permits the reader to appreciate his faults first-hand, and to recognize just how limited his perception of events is. We are suspicious of Rodríguez's constant presence in Lino's house long before the latter is told of his wife's unfaithfulness, especially after his dream in which Don Ano-Ano proposes hypothetically Rodríguez's deception of the unsuspecting Doménech. The reader is aware of Lino's tendency to rationalize in order to avoid blame. He has always wanted to go it alone in business and in marriage. Ironically, at the end he is crushed by the weight of his self-inflicted loneliness, for his pride has prevented him from accepting his wife's desire to accompany him in his suffering. He realizes too late that human relationships must be mutually sustained. His call for mercy at the end recalls various allusions to the theme of grace: in the scene of the crime, High Grace, and the title of the last chapter, "Sad Grace." Perhaps the best comment on Lino's plight, as we usually see in Ayala's fictions, is a question which appears in the novel. In reply to Lino's inquiry about Pinedo's end, the priest of San Cosme asks at the beginning of the novel: "Couldn't human grace have intervened like divine grace to avoid such tremendous suffering?" (1035).

CHAPTER 8

Abductions, Rapes and Other Inconveniences

U NDER the unusual title *De raptos, violaciones y otras inconveniencias (About Abductions, Rapes and Other Inconveniences)*, Ayala published in 1966 a novelette together with four shorter fictions which had appeared separately three years before in a volume called *El As de Bastos (The Ace of Clubs)* with one additional story, "El prodigio" ("The Prodigy"). In this chapter we shall treat all of these selections since they belong to the same period and involve varied forms of outrage. In his prologue to *The Ace of Clubs*, the Argentine novelist H. A. Murena speaks of Ayala's depiction of "terrible human nature." We should attenuate this remark, however, by offering the alternative of "terrible human weakness" since our author does not condemn man in general. There are, to be sure, some stories that are in diverse degrees scandalous, atrocious, and perhaps even scabrous in content; this in itself is a formidable challenge to a writer as concerned with aesthetics as Ayala is. His mastery of his media is evident as he enlists irony, subtlety, ambiguity, humor, and superb verbal agility to make scenes of this sort neither offensive nor vulgar. This is particularly true of the short novel *El rapto (The Abduction)*, one of our author's most polished artistic achievements.

I   *"El As de Bastos" ("The Ace of Clubs")*

"The Ace of Clubs" is introduced by no less than five literary quotations from Ovid, Garcilaso de la Vega, Shakespeare, Ronsard, and Quevedo, alluding to the brevity of the flower and exhorting us to enjoy it in its prime. Ayala's version of the same theme on a much more prosaic plane involves a chance meeting (like that of Vatteone and Nelly in "Meeting") of Bastos, whose name we

88

must translate to Clubs in order to appreciate the title, and Matilde. Both are on their way in winter to a beach resort which was the scene of a frustrated extramarital summer romance many years before. Clubs, now a widower, and Matilde, a divorcee, discuss the desires they did not fulfill and the opportunities not taken as their train moves "as in dreams, across the frozen fields"—a fitting background to their sentimental journey of emotions killed by the frost of time. Their reminiscences seem to belong to an age long past: *"in illo tempore"*, "a thousand years ago", "a century and a half." References to classical deities heighten the irony of the deterioration wrought by time: Clubs, the swimming "ace" who was like a young Triton suffering Tantalus's torture before Matilde's attraction, now appears to her like "an old dummy," and the graceful Nereid Matilde is best described by lines from Rodrigo Caro's famous seventeenth-century "Elegy to the Ruins of Itálica" which Clubs repeats to himself. His memories of a Matilde of marble, alabaster, and gold yield to the vision of a "plump hand covered with rings."

This time, however, they avail themselves of the opportunity at a local hotel where they waste no time in going to bed, but each is profoundly shaken by the experience, for Clubs finds that despite Matilde's insistence that she had often imagined him in her husband's place, her interest was strictly generic—in what she laughingly calls "the Ace of Clubs," and he is further irked to hear her sigh for her ex-husband. Matilde, in turn, is deeply distressed by the sight of her sleeping lover as she contemplates the "mortal paleness of the dummy, the eyes sunken in the bottom of the black sockets, and the dry mouth" (1189).[1]

Ayala's story illustrates with sadness the old poetical theme of love's ripe moment and adds to it the element of death, for here memories are "ashes." The final description of Clubs recalls the seventeenth-century author Mira de Amescua's drama *El esclavo del demonio (The Devil's Slave)* in which Don Gil, trading his soul for the opportunity of enjoying his desired Leonor, finds that the woman he embraces is a skeleton covered with a clock. Our author's twentieth-century version of that transformation needs no supernatural intervention: the devil is *time*.

What is obviously a very difficult and potentially scabrous scene is discreetly rendered by the art of metaphor, circumlocution, and omission. Ayala's story shows the contemporary degradation of values which has divested love of traditional poetic and romantic notions by reducing it to eroticism and phallic cult, for which—it must be noted—woman seems to bear much responsibility. The narrator takes the part of each character by means of indirect dialogue, but during the moment of crisis retreats to observe with detachment the excesses of the "good woman" and Clubs. At the end, however, he shares his creatures' anguish, observing not with the moralist's scorn, but with the humanist's pity, "the unfortunate woman" and "poor Clubs."

II   *"Una boda sonada"* (*"A Resounding Wedding"*)

"A Resounding Wedding," 1962, clearly demonstrates that a good story stems not only from what is told but also from the way it is told. Here, Ayala uses a veil of language which is as effective in concealing vulgarity as the veils which the feminine protagonist uses to cover herself in her seductive dance.

The story seems to retell a lyrical idyll about a refined provincial poet and an exquisitely sensitive artist whose souls meet "in a desert of vulgarity," bringing about the poet's chivalrous offer of marriage as public reparation for the unjust ridicule of her audience. Beneath this veil of embroidered rhetoric, however, is really a story of an ode-writing provincial newspaper reporter who marries a modest (and surprisingly virtuous) variety show dancer who answers the jeers of her vulgar public in an equally vulgar, but most appropriate way.

The rivalry between the "sensitive artist" whose *nom de guerre* is Flor del Monte and the less spiritual Creole of Fire becomes a war between "spirit" and "matter." Eventually, it extends to the whole city and leads to the insults of some fellows "entrenched" in their theater boxes. Flor answers their jeers with a volley of "explosive detonation, like the devil in the *Divina Comedia, avea del cul fatto trombetta"* [sounding his rear like a trumpet] (1197).[2] One must concede that the dancer's loud expression of flatulence so elegantly described by our author is an obnoxious answer to her attackers; however, as Flor del Monte suggests, it is not as noxious as the firearm that it substitutes.

The themes of love and death intertwine as the poet Homero (named for the immortal Homer, of course) Ataíde metaphorically carries in his nickname Ataúde, the casket *(ataúd)* which is at the same time a reminder of his father's modest mortuary firm and a

memento mori. It is suspected that funeral flowers form his romantic bouquets, and after he marries another flower *(Flor)* in the
"dead" provincial capital, white funeral horses lead the wedding
coach. The retired dancer then realizes her spiritual potential in the
"divinatory arts," using her same costume to take the place of her
husband's Aunt Amancia, alias "Celestial Messenger," who had
been able to predict her own death with such accuracy that she
simply lay down in her coffin. An official autopsy was not so easily
avoided, however, and the cryptic comment *Sic transit gloria mundi*
(equivalent to "thus pass the glories of the world") may equally be
applied to the whole noisy incident, for indeed, the glorious deeds
of the past are soon forgotten, the only reminder being the name of
the first Ataíde child—Santiago—for the Apostle Saint James,
celebrated in Galicia as "The Son of Thunder." Another burlesque
insinuation occurs in the review of the resounding wedding written
by Ataíde and published in the pages of *The Echo of the Nation*,
which, in view of the nature of the event, provides a grotesque comment on the national reality it echoes.

III   *"Violación en California" ("Rape in California")*

While many male characters in Ayala's fictions, starting with
Tragicomedy of a Man Without a Spirit, are entrapped by practical
jokes, his women often seem to be more aggressive and dangerous.
"Rape in California," 1961, presents two versions of the theme of
female lasciviousness, one inspiring laughter and the other horror.

Police Lieutenant E. A. Harter tells his wife Mabel how a young
traveling salesman (so often the seducer-protagonists of coarse
jokes) was raped by two female hitchhikers who, after satisfying
"their libidinous demands," disappeared while their victim ran into
the arms of the police. The real humor is in the details that the
police officer describes and in the switch in usual roles. As Harter
explains: "You can imagine, Mabel, that for technical reasons, raping a man is much more difficult than raping a woman" (1207). The
poor victim would have complied gladly if he had not been intimidated by their pistols, but it was evident that violence was
precisely what the young women liked. Ayala indirectly uses the
psychological artifice of inhibiting our tendency to laugh as Harter
tries to halt the joking of his subordinates; the police lieutenant sees
it as an alarming sign of the times and not as a funny incident.

Mabel, strangely enough, is not as surprised as her experienced policeman husband and in fact counters with the story of the two López sisters who lived in the town of Santa Cecilia (ironically this saint was a virgin and martyr) in New Mexico. During the war, when most men were in Europe, the sisters lured the town idiot to their house in order to explore *"in anima vili"* (in an inferior animal) the "anatomical particularities of the human male" (1209). When the object of the idiot's visits threatened to become known, the "modest vestals" killed him with a cake containing pieces of glass, but the crime was never so proved as to implicate them. Harter realizes that his wife's story shows that "there is nothing new under the California sun."

Mabel's anecdote is anything but humorous probably because it involves murder and people whom she identifies as residents of her home town while her husband's story seems relatively funny because of the protagonists' anonymity and distance from the narrator. The humor implicit in such role changes recalls that of a short farce by Quevedo, "El Marión," which Ayala comments upon in one of his essays.[3] In this farce Quevedo exposes the ridiculousness of social forms concerned with honor in seventeenth-century Spain by putting the man in the place of the courted woman whose virtue formed the base of family honor.

The atrocity committed by the López sisters may reflect those aberrations which appear in times of war and international distress, but the rape of the salesman is an act of gratuitous malevolence. As a postscript to our author's acknowledgement that incidents like these are nothing new under the sun, soon after his story was completed, a news report of a similar rape of a male was published in Puerto Rico, so as we can see, there is no end to the story.

IV   *"Un pez"* (*"A Fish"*)

The anecdote presented in "A Fish," 1963, is, as the narrator acknowledges at the end, a story which actually appeared in the *New York Times,* but Ayala elaborates upon it and opens it to further interpretation as possibly another "sign of the times" like "Rape in California."[4] The narrator, a Polish immigrant, explains how, alone in his apartment, staring at the empty street while indulging his favorite pastime—doing nothing—he was offered a fish by five young fellows "manning" an old white Lincoln convertible which looked like "a sort of bathtub." He did not refuse and found himself the owner of an enormous, dead, foul-smelling fish, which elicited several insults from his wife. The police considered it his responsibility to pay for its removal, and the narrator attributes his being the butt of jokes to envy because of the publicity he received in the *Times*.

Andrés Amorós suggests some undetermined symbolism which leaves the reader guessing. The dead fish, ritually delivered in a white (sacred color) vehicle by five men dressed in white T-shirts who could thus symbolically act as priests, may very well be an animal totem which reflects the passivity of the narrator—and indirectly, of his society—content to watch television all day, complain about the world and its problems, let things happen, and do nothing.[5] The fish may also be seen as an erotic symbol as in Ayala's vanguard story "Dead Hour," for it turns out to be as disagreeable a surprise as the earlier visit of his lascivious neighbor Doña Rufa which he describes. Too weak to say no, the protagonist in both cases gets something that he does not bargain for. Much of the humor of "A Fish" lies in the tremendous seriousness of the narrator, who like the victim of the previous story, is too involved in his tale to appreciate its comic aspects.

V   *"El prodigio" ("The Prodigy")*

An epitaph in German which precedes "The Prodigy," 1961, and the setting of the story over two centuries ago provide a distant and legendary atmosphere for this myth. It is the sad history of a prodigious child, ambiguously named "Félix or Fénix," whose genius in the most diverse subjects has attracted the protection of the kind priest of his small town. The priest brings Fénix to the attention of the prince's architect who is working on a new convent there and the latter takes the child to the palace where he is dressed in a pink silk cossack with lace, allowed to "perform" at chess and recitation, and then left forgotten in the servants' quarters. The architect finally takes him back home again where the boy continues to languish and is ultimately killed by a she-hog.

The horrible fate of the brilliant child is another example of Ayala's comment upon the autopsy performed on Amancia in "A Resounding Wedding"—*Sic transit gloria mundi*. This is further underscored by the priest's epitaph predicting future fame, ironically erased by time, and now only remembered by the omniscient narrator of the story.

Ayala has called "The Prodigy" an "allegory of the mortal

world," an evaluation which would seem to support the above interpretation but, as is usual in our author's work, it is a dense fiction
which opens many avenues of conjecture.[6] It may be seen as a commentary on the uncertain destiny of genius in society, fruitlessly
consumed because it is not appreciated. The implication seems to
be that Nature destroys its gifts and men help to bring the destruction about. The nineteenth-century Spanish novelist Cecilia Böhl de
Faber, better known as Fernán Caballero, is reputed as saying that
intelligence is a luxury, sometimes useless, sometimes fatal, and we
might well add—sometimes both. The uncertainty of the child's
names shows that they may be diversely viewed as fortune—Félix—or misfortune—Fénix, the mythological bird that
allows itself to be consumed by fire and then, in accordance to an
eternal cycle, arises from the ashes. Our genius is a seventh child, a
fact which is also of uncertain portent since the number seven is
both fatal and felicitous in superstition. The play on names is also
an allusion to the genius of Spanish Golden Age theater, Lope Félix
de Vega Carpio, popularly known as "el Fénix de los ingenios" (the
Phoenix of Ingenuity) and called by Cervantes "el monstruo de la
naturaleza" (nature's monster). Lope, unlike little Fénix, died in old
age, but he was stricken with great sorrow during his life because of
the misfortunes of his children and his lovers, so it may be said that
he, like Ayala's Fénix, suffered greatly. Interestingly enough, in a
volume called *Posthumous Fame,* edited by Lope's follower Mon-
talbán, a hundred fifty-three writers praised his genius. Does this
Phoenix rise from the ashes in different ages and climes as is
suggested by the use of Italian, an epitaph in German, and an allusion to a Spanish dramatist?

The story points out the unfortunate destiny of genius in serving
as spectacle and entertainment, for even such appreciative souls as
the well-meaning priest and architect have no idea of the purpose of
so much intelligence that is neither specialized nor practical. Fénix's
fate is the same as that of the anachronistic chess-playing robot
which had been the court sensation some years before, and is now in
ruins. We are reminded by the way the "wise monkey" (as the
architect affectionately calls him) is dressed in the court of the
pathetic dwarf-buffoons who appear in paintings by Velázquez of
the Habsburgs' court. The theme of genius on display has literary
precedents in Cervantes's exemplary novel *El licenciado Vidriera*
(The Brilliant Man of Glass) and Galdós's novel *Torquemada en la*
hoguera (Torquemada in the Fire).

Also traditional in Spanish letters is the use of the pig as a symbol of bestiality and vulgarity, for example, in Cervantes's *Don Quijote* and Mateo Alemán's picaresque novel of the same period, *Guzmán de Alfarache*. More than an animal atrocity, however, Fénix's death represents a human atrocity similar to that which occurs in Camilo José Cela's 1942 novel *La familia de Pascual Duarte (The Family of Pascual Duarte)* where a poor, neglected, idiot child is killed by a pig. In Ramón del Valle-Inclán's novel *Tirano Banderas (Tyrant Banderas)*, another child is partially eaten by a pig. Ironically, in Ayala's story, the mother earlier feeds the child bacon from a pig. The narrator comments succinctly toward the end that "everyone knows that the pig, an omnivorous animal like man, eats anything" (1223).

VI   *"El rapto" ("The Abduction")*

In spite of explicit hints found in the text of *The Abduction*, 1965, some critics did not realize that the novel is a reelaboration of Chapter LI of the first part of the *Quijote* in which the goatherd, Eugenio, after chasing a runaway female goat and lamenting the fickleness of women, stops to tell his story to Don Quijote and his friends. He had been courting Leandra, when a flashy, arrogant soldier named Vicente de la Roca (Rosa in the first edition of the *Quijote*), returning from the wars in Italy, fascinated the young lady so that she ran away with the attractive stranger only to be robbed by him and abandoned in a cave. The abductor, however, had left her physically intact, respecting that "jewel which once lost, leaves no hope of ever being recuperated." Ayala, commenting upon the episode in his essay "La invención del *Quijote*" ("The Invention of the *Quijote*"), says that this unexplainable "continence of the youth" is paradoxically the worst possible insult to the lady's lasciviousness.[7]

The Abduction begins with an introduction which provides a present-day reference. The narrator who, like Ayala, lives in New York, chats on a train with some young people returning to Spain from jobs in Germany where the narrator has also been traveling. The introduction prefigures some aspects of the story which follows, notably with regard to characters, the theme of honor, and the ease with which the historical past is forgotten. The story itself revives a forgotten lesson from the *Quijote*.

Vicente de la Roca, retaining his Cervantine name and surrounded by literary allusions to Góngora and Garcilaso de la Vega, suddenly appears in a small town, as though out of a legendary past, flaunting a flashy motorcycle and a Grundig radio which leave the young fellows of the town envious. Vicente, who has come from Germany where he was working, makes friends with Patricio who confides to him his romantic interest in Julita. Since the girl has kept him and his friend Fructuoso guessing, he asks Vicente to sound her out, but dazzled by the stranger, Julita runs away with him. Like the Cervantine Leandra, she is robbed and abandoned—in a hotel—but, to her father's relief, she retains intact that "jewel that once lost, leaves no hope of ever being recuperated." The inconsolable Patricio goes hunting with Fructuoso in a pastoral setting evoked by quotes from Garcilaso de la Vega's eclogues, and the two friends lament the incident. Patricio, however, receives a letter from Vicente, explaining that his only motive was to show him that the inconstant Julita was not worth his friend's attention and that Patricio is wasting his talent in such a small town. He urges him impatiently to join him, and promises that the stolen jewels will be returned to Julita.

The structure of the story itself is not linear, but rather consists of numerous flashbacks and versions of the same incidents magnificently orchestrated by the author into a harmonious work of narrative art. The plurality of perspectives offered in the novel leaves the reader to judge for himself as to the motives of each character. Julita becomes a much more complicated person than Cervantes's Leandra, as in a typically Ayalan fashion she examines her conscience in an attempt to explain her conduct. Her assessment of the experience contrasts enormously with that of Vicente in his letter to Patricio, and even with that of her father whose only concern is her virginity.

Whereas Chapter LI of the *Quijote* offers no explanation at all for the strange conduct of Vicente, Ayala's novel, while maintaining the basic ambiguity of the original, lends itself at least to inference. The key to the mystery lies in Ayala's brilliant study of another Cervantine work, "El curioso impertinente" ("The Impertinent Curiosity-Seeker") which is incorporated into the *Quijote* just as Eugenio's story is. This little "exemplary novel" has never been explained in a satisfactory way, and the reason why Anselmo uses his friend Lothario to test his wife's honor is a continuing enigma. Ayala's study of the problem convincingly shows that Anselmo's action represents the sublimation of homosexual instincts. By fostering the union of his friend with his wife, he hopes to achieve vicarious satisfaction in view of the oneness of man and wife in Christian marriage, spelled out by the Council of Trent. Ayala's solution to the Anselmo enigma is applicable to the Vicente de la Roca mystery, and using one Cervantes story to illuminate another is justified in view of our author's own assertion that various novelettes found in the *Quijote* are interrelated as modulations of the theme of Eros.[8]

Curiously, male critics of *The Abduction*, like Alberto Sánchez, Adrián García Montoro, and Keith Ellis,[9] see Vicente as a well-intentioned friend, while Rosario Hiriart and this author[10] find more than enough reasons to suspect Vicente's homosexuality as the cause of the unconsummated abduction: subtle allusions to his "little moustache," polished nails, big ring, and little suitcase tied with a bow; his insistent aversion to women in general; his exaggerated contempt toward Julita; overdoing the expression "dear Patricio" in his letter to the point where it no longer seems rhetorical; and finally, in the impatience with which he gives Patricio the ultimatum of joining him or it will be the last time he disappoints him. As we have noted, there is no evidence in the *Quijote* of this possibility, except perhaps in Cervantes's own vacillation regarding Vicente's last name, between the effeminate-sounding Rosa (Rose) and the manly Roca (Rock), suggesting strength. As is often the case in our day, Vicente's prestige seems based predominantly upon the vehicle he rides, for the flashy motorcycle represents his virility. Half man and half motorcycle, he is like a twentieth-century centaur, mythological abductor, but when he leaves his vehicle to be with Julita in the hotel for a moment, he obviously poses no threat to her honor.

As Ayala has recognized, the novel can be read and enjoyed even though the reader may not be aware that it represents a reworking of a chapter of the *Quijote* or that numerous allusions to Spanish and universal literature are encrusted in the text. A complete appreciation of Ayala's creative artistry, however, requires an awareness of all of the literary elements which make *The Abduction* not only a delightful and extraordinary novel, but also a very original way of commentating upon Cervantes's work and, of course, of paying a tribute to the creator of the modern novel.

CHAPTER 9

Essays on Social Themes

IN a revealing essay entitled "El fondo sociológico de mis
novelas" ("The Sociological Background of My Novels") written
in 1968, Ayala comments upon the propensity of the critics to look
for his sociological ideas in the plots of his fictions.[1] Although he ad-
mits that critics should detect and situate these ideas, they should
do so with the purpose of establishing the function of these ideas
within the structure of the work, for while ideas are an essential element of the intellectual content which we commonly call plot, they
do not determine the worth of literary art. Our author objects to
categorizing *Dog's Death* as a political satire because this label only
points out the obvious materials of construction while ignoring what
interests the artist fundamentally in this novel: the social and moral
implications which result from the acts of individual characters who
find themselves caught within these circumstances. Neither the
totalitarian dictatorship of *Dog's Death* nor the democracy depicted
in *The Bottom of the Glass* is under scrutiny as a political system except to the extent that these circumstances create an environment
presenting diverse conditions of duress conducive to exposing
aspects of human behavior. Concrete circumstances always exert
pressure on individuals, pushing them toward the interior of conscience in the direction of self-reflection which Ayala regards as the
supreme moment of morality.

His novels, then, address themselves to social morality, treating
power as a necessary evil which "should be organized in such a way
that it is reduced to the indispensable minimum."[2] Thus, while the
examination of ideas is an important part of literary study, it must
be integrated with the implications of these ideas in the actual texture of the novels, and with evaluations of an aesthetic nature. In
another essay, "Función social de la literatura" ("Social Function of
Literature"), Ayala indicates that despite changing vogues in the art
of writing, the quality of literature finally depends upon aleatory

98

factors such as the innate genius of the artist to structure and articulate his intuitions.[3]

The strong interrelation between our author's prolific production in the political and social sciences, literary criticism, and his fictions is a theme which has been studied at length.[4] In order to show how Ayala's essentially coherent view of life conditions his expression in both genres—the essay and the novel—we shall deal briefly with his principal books of essays of social themes with special attention to aspects which elucidate his use of some of these materials in his fictions. While there is an inherent injustice in reducing whole books of carefully developed essays to brief paraphrased summaries, it is the only procedure applicable in these limited pages and is more than justified by the value of these works in themselves and their usefulness in achieving a fundamental understanding of our author's inventions.

In the preface to *Hoy ya es ayer (Today Is Already Yesterday)*, a compilation of three previously published books of essays, Ayala comments in 1971 upon the basic congruence of his attitudes in his political and social writings through the years.[5] He notes, however, that there is variance in the material offered by the incessant alteration of historical circumstances and by his progressive abandonment of academic formalism. Indeed, the reader can perceive his disdain for super-specialization, implicit in the non-technical language and non-academic format, dispensing with the documentary apparatus, and lending a tone of personal concern.

I Tratado de sociología (Treatise on Sociology)

Intended mainly for university students, Ayala's *Treatise on Sociology*, the most academic of his discursive works, appeared in Buenos Aires in 1947 in a three volume edition. It was subsequently reedited in 1959, forming one monumental volume which requires for its full appreciation some sociological preparation; hence we shall limit our comments to several points of interest which are developed in his personal essays and in his fictions, remitting the reader to the book itself for possible further study.

Our author's attitude toward his field is that knowledge should work in function of present-day life, and that it is difficult to apply traditional scientific methods to the social "sciences" since they deal with situations wherein the individual human conscience plays a role. His attention to specific instances of individual interaction is manifested in Chapter II of the first part of the book in which he analyzes sociological experience via the concrete example in which two strangers meet. He is fully aware of the fact that the confrontation of two individual consciences for the first time constitutes one of the perennial, inexhaustible, and eternal experiences of poetic creation—at the same time trivial and potentially profound. The reader of Ayala's fictions can observe the character of these meetings in *Dog's Death* and corroborate how class consciousness comes into play; in other works, such as "Meeting" and "The Ace of Clubs," the reader can discover reencounters which are equally interesting.

In Chapter IV of the same section, Ayala examines the sociological phenomenon of fashion, ever-changing and corresponding to the conditions of society. This theme is again developed by our author more than twenty-five years later in a recent work entitled "Todo el año (literalmente) carnaval" ("Carnival All Year Long [Literally]").

The Second Part of the *Treatise* studies specific aspects of man's life in society in a state of evolution propelled by free will. The author considers as one of his major contributions to sociology, which he calls a "science of crisis," his concept of crisis as an identifiable situation marked by the disruption of the natural rhythm of life and by the unforeseeable nature of events. This atmosphere of crisis is clearly discernible as the background of *Dog's Death*, and is present to some degree in *The Bottom of the Glass*.

Also in this part, Ayala treats the crises of adolescence and youth with regard to the progressive adjustment of fantasies and desires to reality and the assumption of responsibility. Similar themes, as we have noted in previous chapters, are elaborated in *Tragicomedy of a Man Without a Spirit*, "Dead Hour" and "Erika Facing Winter." Ayala differentiates civilizational processes, which are present in society as a whole, from cultural processes, which include language, custom, and art. He sees law, with its necessary involvement in spiritual structures, as a system which articulates both. In many of his personal essays, there is an abiding interest in Hispanic culture in conjunction with more general references to Western culture.

II   El problema del liberalismo (The Problem of Liberalism)[6]

In *The Problem of Liberalism*, Ayala states that freedom is an unconditional component of man's dignity, for without it, he loses the essence of his human condition and is degraded to animalism. Freedom makes possible the change we call history, whereas animal life is marked by constant repetition. Since freedom is established within a social order, it is always exposed to risks, and its defense requires enormous moral energy and vigilance. The rights of the individual in mass society should be the cardinal concern of political philosophy, for without it, man cannot raise himself from biological animalism toward the sphere of the spirit.

Freedom, says Ayala, may be curtailed indiscriminately by the tyranny of dictators or that of the masses. Technology must not be used to enslave man, but rather to serve him. Ayala optimistically considers human reason capable of realizing its errors and rectifying them; thus, the whole problem of freedom is essentially a moral one.

Reiterating that our author's inventions are not to be construed as simple illustrations of sociological concepts, it is nevertheless fruitful to consider how the presence of these materials in his novels is determined by immanent relationships between characters, so that they are authentic literary developments and not extra-novelistic adjuncts. The degradation of which Ayala speaks in *The Problem of Liberalism* is suggested by the persistent animalistic imagery in *Dog's Death* and *The Bottom of the Glass* where first dictatorial, and then mercantile tyranny exert pressure upon characters who must come to terms with their circumstances and their conscience. The moral aspect of man's being reduced to animalism may be adduced in the actual presence of animals throughout Ayala's inventions, allusions in the form of metaphors or gestures (Sara Gross's canine gesture at the close of "The Last Supper"), hedonism ("The Ace of Clubs," and newer works such as "Dialogues of Love"), gluttony ("The Ailing King"), and in other scenes of conduct actuated by sensual appetites only and not by intellectual or moral considerations. His faith in the possibility of individual rectification and progress may be observed in the many examples his works offer of characters who "touch bottom" in their examination of the recesses of their conscience in *The Abduction, Dog's Death, The Bottom of the Glass*, "The Lamb's Head," "The Tagus," etc.

III   Razón del mundo (The World Explained)[7]

Ayala's chief concern in this collection of essays, first published in 1944, is the responsibility of the intellectual in today's world. This invites a consideration of how knowledge should be used to nurture progress by carrying out a constant reexamination of history which not only includes past events but also "apocryphal memories" forged by the imagination or in other words, fiction.

Our times, says Ayala, demand the reconsideration of the intellectual's role in society which approaches the fundamental question of the relationship of the spirit to that society. The prestige which accompanied intellectual pursuits in the past century has yielded to hostility and pressures to control them. Recognizing that complete objectivity is impossible, our author sees as the intellectual's responsibility the task of observing the whole panorama of events in order to form theories relevant to real problems and experiences without becoming excessively compromised in the play of conflicting forces.

In contrast to former centuries when the work of intellectuals was considered more important than the personality of those who created it, the cult of originality has supplanted even esteem for the intrinsic value of art. Universal artistic tradition sought new aesthetic expression for the same materials which had been used previously by other authors. Surprise in plot was to be avoided as an element interfering with the aesthetic emotion.

These ideas help explain Ayala's artistic reworking of traditional plots and materials in new structures and contexts in accord with his own untransferable experiences and the circumstances provided by today's world. It should be recalled that in *The Usurpers*, he not only uses well-known historical examples, but to avoid surprise, he provides summaries of the plots at the beginning of the selections. "A Story by Maupassant" points out the inevitability of plot repetition, and the indignation of the two women upon seeing each other in identical dress reflects a similar attitude on the part of many authors today when they coincide in their ideas, a situation which our author finds lamentable.

The proletarization of intellectuals has forced them to yield to special interest groups which may be powerful. The masses esteem intelligence only as technical knowledge or if it produces practical and tangible results. Yet the common man of mass society suffers psychic devastation in not being able to direct his conduct toward the achievement of programs and ideas—a uniquely human necessity—in times of crisis when unpredictable conditions reduce his existence to an "infra-human level." The intellectual himself is caught up in the crisis and is "paralyzed" by it, unable to view events from an independent position or to distinguish his theoretical convictions from practical interests. Certainly the reader will recognize this as the world of *Dog's Death* where so many events are subject to the caprices of Bocanegra, and where Pinedo, who considers himself an intellectual, is not only paralyzed literally and figuratively, but becomes embroiled in the very situation he denounces.

The second part of *The World Explained* is concerned with "The Hispanic Perspective." Ayala exonerates Spanish culture of responsibility for the spiritual catastrophe which afflicts the West because of Spain's marginal influence in the development of Occidental affairs since it retreated into its own Counter Reformation in the sixteenth century. The failure of existing systems creates a juncture favorable to Spain's potential role in fomenting a spiritual regeneration of the West in accordance with universal principles inoperative since the Renaissance which have been preserved virtually intact in the Hispanic culture. The personality of Saavedra Fajardo (1584 - 1648) provides an example of a dissident conscience which still remained faithful to the idea of a world guided by moral principles, in contrast to the Machiavellianism then rampant.

In other essays in the book, Ayala supports change as the basic character of history and affirms that "restorations" of former models offer no solutions to present problems. He also pronounces himself in favor of eliminating a folkloric vision of Spain in order to accentuate universal aspects of Hispanic culture which would permit its greater international influence. He concludes that new solutions may be forthcoming if intellectuals are allowed to operate in a liberal order organized with freedom as society's principal criterion.

IV   La crisis actual de la enseñanza
(The Present Crisis in Education)[8]

In this group of essays, Ayala addresses himself to the problem of the deterioration of academic preparation and the overcrowding of facilities in Argentina and the United States. While a possible solution for Argentina may be restricting college entrance to well-qualified students, extensive university reform is needed to reflect social transformation and to improve intellectual and technical preparation in order to better serve the needs of our times. These essays were published in 1959 but are not at all obsolete.

Because education in Argentina and other Western countries reflects the increasing Americanization of the world, an examination of the mode of teaching perfected in the United States provides the most obvious example of the direction in which education is headed. Ayala describes the shock which United States educators received when they realized the gigantic scientific strides advanced by the Soviet Union in a relatively short time. The failure of American education according to our author stems from a faulty understanding of John Dewey's ideas; student interest is interpreted as student entertainment. Rousseau changed the traditional authoritarian approach to one of creative study, but his concepts require exceptional teachers to be effectively implemented as well as an adaptation of the noble savage idea to a civilized environment.

Putting its hopes for social advancement in education, the family, during recent times, has ceded its authority to the school so that "junior" has become not only king of the house, but also the tyrant of the school. The lack of sanctions and authority against which healthy children need to rebel in order to develop into responsible adults is a void filled all too often by gangs which impose their own absurd and strict discipline, resulting in juvenile delinquency and social disintegration.

This laxity toward youthful transgressions is seen in the permissive attitude of the newspapers toward Junior Rodríguez and the gangs in *The Bottom of the Glass* and in "The Hoodlums Again," which we shall discuss in Chapter 11. In his essay about the educational crisis, Ayala does not recommend a return to traditional molds, but sees the need for intensified spiritual and material preparation of the masses, utilizing the advances of technology and integrating the schools with social reality.

V   Tecnología y libertad (Technology and Freedom)[9]

This work and the two books of essays which follow are included in Ayala's book *Los ensayos: Teoría y crítica literaria (Essays: Literary Theory and Criticism)* under the heading of "The Writer and His World." They are presented in this chapter because they deal with social problems more than purely literary ones.

With distinct echoes of José Ortega y Gasset's *La rebelión de las masas (The Rebellion of the Masses)*, Ayala poses the question of who dominates the chaos of our world in which international relations have turned into crises and man feels demoralized by the disorder which surrounds him. Colossal technical progress, unaccompanied by an adequate moral base, has placed the individual in an impersonal world which threatens his freedom by trying to incorporate him into the vast machine of the State.

In the nineteenth century and before, the State was primarily empowered to declare war and make peace, but now it has a hand in every aspect of social, economic, and even artistic life. History records collective events, but individual development depends in great part on the moral decisions made by each person's conscience which must function in an atmosphere of freedom. Public opinion, therefore, should be enlightened by a free press whose duty is to inform. The press has abdicated this role and, given to sensationalism, tends to manipulate public opinion and to degrade the intelligence of the masses. Mass democracy can easily turn into mass totalitarianism which may take the outward form of exaggerated nationalism.

Ayala suggests that values be reformulated to make them apt for present-day circumstances in a more liberal state. Until then, we are likely to see further manifestations of crisis such as the degradation of language into insults which, like infra-human cries, represent the degeneration of language no longer useful in promoting understanding. This mark of crisis abounds in the insults and offensive gestures found in our author's fictions "The Tagus," "Monkey Story," "A Resounding Wedding," "A Fish," and in his more recent "Dialogues of Love."

VI   El escritor en la sociedad de masas
(The Writer in Mass Society)[10]

The place of the man of letters in today's society, his mission, and his public are problems analyzed in *The Writer in Mass Society*, 1956. "For whom do we write?" asks Ayala, and more specifically: "I, a Spaniard in America, for whom do I write?" The writer who carries out his work in exile from his native land not only loses his natural reading audience, but is by circumstance inhibited in what he may write about his host country. In a larger sense, however, all writers are essentially exiled, having been alienated from the rest of the society by the loss of that prestige once accorded the intellectual in the past. Facing this difficulty, the man of letters has as his mission the task of probing life with complete freedom which may have intellectual, moral, and cultural implications, and of trying to

awaken analogous intuitions in his readers. He works for a con-
tinuous revision of life's meaning for the community with an
awareness of present-day reality. His freedom must not be curtailed
in any way by intervention from the State which produces sterility
in art.

Ayala suggests that writers try to foment a healthy culture for the
masses by creating great art accessible to all. This does not mean
simplification of art, but rather the creation of works which are
complex enough to be appreciated on various levels, like *Hamlet*
which in addition to other things may be enjoyed as a "truculent
melodrama," and the *Quijote* with its easily appreciated clownlike
comedy. Works of this type, which provide a variety of possible
modes of access, are capable of appealing to the more noble instincts of the masses and of elevating them intellectually, spiritually, and aesthetically while the other alternative of over-
simplification would lower literary quality and degrade the masses.
Our author's attitude implies, of course, a fundamental faith in the
ability of the masses to grow intellectually.

Some of the themes which Ayala discusses in this book appear in
his fictions. The plight of the exiled writer is woven into the texture
of his novel *Dog's Death* in the case of the Spanish newspaperman
Camarasa whose writings are construed as a criticism of his
"generous" host country and lead to his assassination. The questions
of fame, public, and purpose are treated fictionally in "A Story by
Maupassant" while many of our author's narrators are conscious of
their role as writers, for example in "The Bewitched," *Dog's Death*,
and *The Bottom of the Glass*. Similar themes occur in some of his
most recent lyrical vignettes. Also discussed in *The Writer in Mass
Society* is the phenomenon of the amorphous society in which the
individual is in a process of disintegration and experiences tremendous loneliness. This is undoubtedly the case in "Music to Die By"
which we shall study in another chapter.

VII   De este mundo y el otro
(About This World and the Other One)[11]

While the suggestive title of this book of essays published in 1963
may bring to mind theological connotations not completely extraneous in view of our author's concern for man's destiny, the essays themselves analyze diverse subjects related to the New World
and the Old. Ayala discusses such themes as definable Spanish

characteristics in terms of stereotypes or realities, the value of individual resistance to social pressures, the fortunate experience of Puerto Rico in being able to determine its own destiny, the dangers of United States appeasement in Cuba, and "healthy nationalism" versus the other extreme represented by Peronism.

An essay which is particularly important in appreciating Ayala's novels *The Bottom of the Glass* and *The Abduction* is "El punto de honor castellano" ("The Castilian Point of Honor"). Here, he censures the absurd concept of male honor dependent upon female behavior, at its apex in the seventeenth century as Spanish theater of that time reflects. Our author argues that unrealistically strict norms were in themselves an irresistible inducement for some women and created a situation in which many fine men were subjected to public degradation or reparation for something for which they had no responsibility. When José Lino Ruiz asks himself in *The Bottom of the Glass:* "If I'm a cuckold, what is she?," he points to an omission which characterizes the age-old Spanish attitude toward the deceived husband of an adulteress.[12] The simplistic interpretation of honor as virginity is satirized in *The Abduction* when Julita's father shows concern only for the physical aspect of his daughter's indiscretion.

In conclusion, it may be said that Ayala's essays, though stimulated by concrete historical points of reference, are not dated by changing conditions or circumstances because, like his literary inventions, they aspire to capture permanent aspects of man's problematical existence.

CHAPTER 10

Essays on Literary Themes

BY his own confession, the activity of Francisco Ayala in the field of literary theory and criticism is intimately related to his writing of fiction: "For me, the practice of criticism comes naturally. Even if I didn't write criticism, I would practice it incessantly as a reader and I would apply it, of course, to my own inventions."[1] Ayala's critical work, which spans his whole career as a writer and has been developed simultaneously with his novels, corresponds to the recommendation we have observed in his sociological essays with regard to the creation of literary works complex enough to be appreciated on various levels. Such literature invites the critic to illuminate spiritual and aesthetic values that might not be perceived by other readers, so that his mission, so to speak, is that of guiding others to more profound layers of meaning.

It is impossible to determine whether the techniques Ayala observes in other authors serve as inspiration for his own creation or whether, on the contrary, he notices certain stylistic devices because he has already used them or because they are in accord with his innate sensitivities. Probably all these factors intervene. What Ayala's studies do reveal is that many of the artistic procedures he uses in his imaginative works are not accidental, but reflect his careful analyses of the works of other writers whom he admires.

The writers with whom Ayala's affinity is most pronounced—Cervantes, Quevedo, Galdós and Unamuno—inspire essays developed in a more organic form while numerous others are treated in studies of a rather occasional nature. To give an idea of the scope and variety of his critical interests, it is useful to mention that they include the Spanish writers Jovellanos, Ventura de la Vega, "Azorín," Valle-Inclán, Antonio Machado, José Ortega y Gasset and José Bergamín; the Spanish-American authors Jorge Luis Borges, Eduardo Mallea, Ezequiel Martínez Estrada and Jaime

Torres Bodet; and finally, authors of other languages: Alberto Moravia, Massimo Bontempelli, Elio Vittorini, Jean Paul Sartre, André Gide, Guy de Pourtalès, Alfred de Vigny, Marcel Proust, Rainer Maria Rilke, Alfred Döblin, Johan Wolfgang Goethe, Thomas Mann, John Dos Passos and George Santayana.

I *Classical Spanish Literature*

It is by no means coincidental that Ayala's most extensive studies in classical Spanish literature treat the two authors with whom he is most often compared: Cervantes and Quevedo. The influence of both can be traced in his work; however, in view of the importance he attributes to each individual novelist's personal use of the genre essentially shaped by Cervantes, we may expect that the vision of life expressed in his novels is uniquely his own.

It comes as no surprise that Ayala's admiration for Cervantes is unsurpassed by that accorded any other writer, classical or modern. As far as he is concerned, Cervantes is the creator of the modern novel, and he admires him not only for the transcendental mission he assigned to the genre, but for the prowess he exhibits in his craft. These factors prompted Ayala to say that "in a sense, all of us who have tried writing novels during four and a half centuries have been rewriting the *Quijote* with more or less success."[2] This statement was not intended to be taken literally, of course, but in any case, our author has defended his opinion convincingly in his essays, and indirectly in his fictions.

In "Un destino y un héroe" ("A Destiny and a Hero"), Ayala stresses the real life position of Cervantes as a "dissident conscience" in a time of cultural disassociation.[3] Don Quijote's system of values, inspired by books of chivalry which represent nostalgia for ideals recently lost, is in conflict with the practical order around him, and is, in any event, superior to it. The *Quijote* reflects the drama of Spain's Quijotesque dedication to the anachronistic and incongruous Counter-Reformation, refusing to adapt to the new order of reality which prevailed in the rest of Europe.

Ayala studies Cervantes's complex technique of multiple perspectives in "La invención del *Quijote*" ("The Invention of the *Quijote*") which is designed to make reality appear more substantive. The theme of human existence in the novel is contingent upon the perspective of a subject who is capable of changing and perceiving universal values in different and varying constellations. For Ayala, the atmosphere of the *Quijote* is the same as that of Cervantes's exemplary novels. All examine the problem of human conduct not in terms of sin with pre-established rules of blame and punishment, but rather of error with its own natural consequences. One of the most problematical factors which Cervantes treats in many different forms is *Eros*. In his conclusion, Ayala again points out the close relationship of the individual, Miguel de Cervantes, and the course of the national community in which his life was inserted in times of decisive historical mutation, adding that he represents one of the most alert literary consciences of all time.

In Ayala's consideration of "Experiencia viva y creación poética" ("Live Experience and Poetic Creation") in Cervantes's masterwork, he offers evidence that the famous scene in which Don Quijote's beard is washed by two young ladies is taken from other sources, providing an excellent opportunity to study the Cervantine procedure of composing with "borrowed materials" which is at the same time a practice of Ayala's. He indicates that it is irrelevant whether materials come from immediate experience or by way of reading which is also a "real" experience of our lives; the decisive factor is the author's ability to revitalize them. Cervantes converts mere "situation," an anecdote involving a practical joke, into a profoundly disturbing experience for the reader who is concerned with Don Quijote. Another example of plot repetition, this time occurring in two Cervantine works, shows how treatment may vary even within the same author. The climate of serious moral concern of the exemplary novel *El celoso extremeño (The Jealous Extremaduran)* is contrasted with the relatively gratuitous petulance of the farce, *El viejo celoso (The Jealous Old Man)*. Ayala's own fictions offer several examples of a basic plot treated in different ways as in the two anecdotes about victimized males which appear in "Rape in California."

The study of "Los dos amigos" ("The Two Friends") has previously been mentioned, applying its original and ingenious explanation of "El curioso impertinente" ("The Impertinent Curiosity-Seeker") of Cervantes to a similar possibility of homosexuality in Vicente de la Roca, the protagonist of Ayala's novel *The Abduction*. What is especially noteworthy, besides the content of the study itself, is our author's attitude toward the theme. He emphasizes that Cervantes does not capitalize on the scandalous aspect as many authors would do, but rather provides, with the utmost subtlety and discretion, all the necessary hints for the wise reader to perceive the reason for the husband's otherwise inexplicable conduct in inciting his best friend to tempt his wife. May we add that although the hints are indeed there, as Ayala proves, it took several centuries for them to be discovered by an especially alert and sagacious critic.

As we can see from these studies, our author singles out for examination aspects of the Cervantine novel which may be found in his own writing: the open scrutiny of human behavior and destiny, the importance of relevance to concrete historical circumstances, the use of multiple perspectives, the problematical theme of *Eros*, the utilization of "borrowed" plot materials, an attitude of experimentation in literary production, and the transformation of the practical joke from a simple anecdote into an experience inspiring the reader's introspection. The Cervantine mold proves apt for Ayala, who achieves his own conformation of the genre, determined by his outlook on life and immersion in circumstances which offer their own particular challenges for a dissident conscience.

In two essays on Quevedo, "Observaciones sobre el *Buscón*" ("Observations on the *Petty Thief*") and "Hacia una semblanza de Quevedo" ("Toward a Biographical Sketch of Quevedo"), Ayala studies an aspect of this author's creation which obviously has special importance for him: the way in which Quevedo conceals his intimate self from his readers. He finds that the only slip by which this almost completely hermetic author gives himself away is the sense of shame and intense embarrassment which at times afflicts the pícaro or rogue and which is incompatible with the otherwise shameless character of Don Pablos in a book generally sparing in emotion. Ayala concedes that there are traps implicit in the search for an author in his works, but infers from his findings that this contradictory sense of shame in the rogue was probably a reiterated experience in Quevedo's life and that his famous satire and cynical impudence was deliberately used as a "smoke screen" to hide a real personal sense of modesty. This is for the essayist the secret of Quevedo's personality, for bad eyesight and lameness probably intensified his innate propensity toward resentment and caused him to cultivate caution, reserve, and cynicism in his relationships. The human body, explains Ayala, poses a constant threat of humiliation since physiological impulses in the "human animal" provide occasions to expose us to ridicule and embarrassment. The task of culture is to spiritualize nature, just as love spiritualizes sex.

Ayala himself is a very hermetic author who conceals his intimacy effectively in his works so that his study of this aspect of Quevedo's production is particularly meaningful. Even though our author has no physical imperfections such as those he points out in Quevedo, he is very conscious of how the body may betray us—sadly, as in the case of María Elena who laments having submitted to Tadeo Requena in *Dog's Death*, or with tragicomic humor, as in the public spectacle provided by Captain Ramírez bereft of his beard ("The Captain's Beard"). We shall see in the next chapter the ultimate test to which Ayala submits his ability to hide himself: the writing of lyrical vignettes which are seemingly autobiographical. Speaking of Quevedo in his essays, Ayala notes—or perhaps confesses—that authors who hide their intimate "I" as Quevedo does must be extremely sensitive.

"Sueño y realidad en el barroco" ("Dream and Reality in the Baroque") analyzes a sonnet by Quevedo which reveals his radical perception of life as simply the progress of death. Whereas Cervantes believes in reality and life, Quevedo, on the other hand, does not. Hence a grotesque senselessness of the world provides a unifying current in his works. Distortion is used as the principal aesthetic technique to communicate this metaphysical annihilation which characterizes Quevedo's literature, and in "Espacio barroco" ("Baroque Space"), Ayala examines one of the classical writer's techniques designed to produce distortion: the subjective manipulation of point of view with relation to our position as observers, near or far, above or below the scene.

In response to critics, namely Enrique Pezzoni and Hugo Rodríguez Alcalá, who stress the negative visions found in our author's fictions, Ayala recognizes in the introduction to *Mis páginas mejores (My Best Pages)* that he could cite the illustrious example of Quevedo, but feels that his use of such materials does not correspond to that of the Golden Age writer.[4] Quevedo uses the grotesque to convey his nihilistic outlook whereas Ayala uses it to strengthen his conception of a moral order. His use brings him closer to Cervantes who also employs "scandalous" materials similarly in his works.

Ayala devotes numerous essays to the picaresque novel, and especially to the *Lazarillo de Tormes* because it is not only the "prototype" of the genre or subgenre, but anticipates in many respects the Cervantine novel. As the "cornerstone for the modern novel," the *Lazarillo* is exceptional in many ways. Its title, with its rhetorical contrast of a singularly ordinary name inserted in a form traditionally reserved for famous personages, created a precedent for the naming of Don Quijote de la Mancha. The prologue is in itself a small masterpiece, providing multiple visions of the Lázaro who at maturity writes his life story, the child Lazarillo, and the real author hidden behind his creation. Noting that many of the materials used in the novel are borrowed from folklore and other sources which he documents, Ayala is amazed at the refinement of the anonymous author's literary prowess in manipulating point of view, in establishing transitions from one narrative person to another, and in achieving comic contrast. The purportedly autobiographical "I" achieves transcendental significance in the *Lazarillo* in that it changes the focal point from incident—what happens—to the person to whom it happens—the protagonist. For the protagonist, the world is filled with ambiguity and ambivalence, especially in the episode of Lazarillo and the squire. The novel elicits questions instead of providing authoritative answers. It reflects the attitudes of the developing middle class in Castile under Carlos I which questioned social and ecclesiastic privilege together with other traditional values in the course of acquiring a consciousness of social mobility related to material prosperity.

Ayala considers the *Lazarillo* unfinished; but even in truncated form it changes what might have been a series of consecutive episodes into an organic narration in which different anecdotes are absorbed into the texture of the novel where they are further developed by psychic processes and introspection. This aspect of the picaresque novel's elaboration may have implications for our author's fiction, in view of the episodic nature of both of his mature long novels, *Dog's Death* and *The Bottom of the Glass*. In these novels, the various extraneous anecdotes and incidents—in themselves interesting—are woven into an organic novelistic structure.

Ayala's note on Mateo Alemán's picaresque novel, the *Guzmán de Alfarache*, shows that a writer's purpose may be grossly distorted by the public, for the readers of the *Guzmán* celebrated the rogue's knavery instead of censuring his actions. All the crudities which appear in the novel were originally intended to incur the reader's disapproval, but the human element won out over the implacable verbal severity of the author's sermons, and his ascetic aims were lost.

Other studies of classical writers treat some of the following themes: the psychological complexity of Calderón de la Barca's *La vida es sueño (Life Is a Dream)*; the motivation of Don Juan's desire to dishonor women in Tirso de Molina's *El burlador de Sevilla (The Seducer of Seville)*; and the Baroque technique of placing one literary work within another in Tirso's *Vergonzoso en palacio (Shy Fellow at the Palace)*, recalling Ayala's insertion of one manuscript within another in "The Bewitched" and *Dog's Death*.

II *Modern Writers: Galdós and Unamuno*

Spain's great nineteenth-century novelist Benito Pérez Galdós and the unclassifiable philosopher, essayist, novelist, poet, and professor Miguel de Unamuno of the "Generation of Ninety-Eight" are obviously the two modern writers with whom Ayala feels a most decided affinity. In his extensive studies of their works, he scrutinizes not so much what they say as how they say it, and studies the ways in which they adapt the novel, as developed by Cervantes, to their own needs. The essays show a prodigious amount of reading but absolutely no pedantry; in fact, there is nothing of the traditional academic apparatus associated with literary studies. All the important data is incorporated into the text itself in such a way that the non-academic reader is not intimidated by the usual erudite documentation, but is rather seduced by the relaxed and readable style of the author.

Ayala's study of Galdós in connection with the question of "realism in literature" focuses on the convenient notion of this novelist as a paradigm of realism. It is inaccurate to associate Galdós's "realism" with the communication of data capable of being corroborated by the senses or with naturalism understood as the objective treatment of repulsive materials. Offering examples taken from a wide range of Galdós's writings, Ayala proves that this novelist like Cervantes sees perceptible reality as filled with intangibles such as fantasy, dreams, and invention. By Galdós's own indication, even his celebrated "natural language" is not a faithful, unelaborated imitation of everyday speech. His so-called realism encompasses the totality of human experience which is the realism of authentic literature of all times.

Another aspect of Galdós's creativity which interests the critic is that of first-person narration. In "Los narradores en las novelas de "Torquemada'" ("Narrators in the 'Torquemada' Novels"), Ayala examines the novelist's implementation of Cervantes's most refined techniques. These include the personal fictionalization of the author, multiple narrators which enrich the illusion of reality, and the projection of characters beyond the confines of the text. "La creación del personaje en Galdós" ("The Creation of Character in Galdós") provides our essayist with the opportunity to examine in Galdós his own preferred procedure of incorporating in a premeditated fashion allusions to literary tradition. These allusions often take the form of names suggestive of literary prototypes, actual quotations "lifted" from other works, and the adaptation of borrowed episodes which the author combines with his individual idiosyncracies and times. This practice adds another dimension to reality but is not "realism" because it does not involve direct observation of materials offered by nature. Ayala adds that using allusions to common treasures of literature as an indispensable frame of reference presumes that readers are capable of recognizing and penetrating them.

The critic also explains some unorthodox means of introducing characters in Galdosian novels. In *El amigo Manso (Our Friend Meekness)*, a character who claims he is non-existent introduces the author and at the end faces his creator to ask him to kill him. This story is, according to Ayala, the original inspiration for Augusto Pérez's confrontation with the author Unamuno in *Niebla (Mist)*, which assumes even greater philosophical significance. Another innovative introduction of character occurs when Don Romualdo, a priest invented by Benina in *Misericordia (Mercifulness)* unexpectedly materializes into a real person, real, of course, on the same plane of imaginary reality in which all the characters of the novel exist.

Ayala defends Galdós against two common accusations which originated with the "Generation of Ninety-Eight," namely careless style and "commonness" of spirit. In "Conmemoración galdosiana" ("Galdosian Commemoration"), he sustains that the novelist's occasional lapses of style are more than compensated for by his successes, especially in imagery, but in any case, it is unfair to judge the value of his creations on the basis of isolated details instead of on the whole complex of aesthetic meanings which form a novel. The second supposed flaw points essentially to that society which the novelist used as the raw materials of his creation and does not take into account his tone and intentions which are anything but commonplace. Galdós's characters are inserted in the "great torso" of their society in contrast to Pío Baroja's characters who are marginal or anti-social; if that society was not heroic, it is not Galdós's fault.

Our author's studies on Galdós emphasize certain factors of Cervantine inspiration which are in accord with Ayala's own views: the novel as an individual, artistic perception of life firmly rooted in society, the use of negative ("naturalistic") materials modulated by the author's compassion toward his creatures, creating works which appeal both to refined spirits and simple folk, introducing multiple narrators and perspectives to enhance novelistic reality, and providing allusions to common literary treasures.

Ayala's studies on Unamuno treat his adaptation of the novelistic genre to fit his own unique needs. In 1914, when Unamuno subtitled his work *Mist "Nivola"* (a word he coined) instead of *"Novela"* (Novel), he proclaimed the right of all writers to reject established formal structures and determinations, for at that time the nineteenth-century European novel still projected its norms upon the literary world. In "El arte de novelar en Unamuno" ("The Art of Writing Novels in Unamuno"), Ayala acknowledges that the novelistic genre is so difficult to define that he will only concede that it offers an interpretation of life in written form, generally meant for solitary reading. Unamuno stresses this aspect of mutual "confession" between the author and solitary reader when he directs *Amor y pedagogía (Love and Pedagogy)* and the prologue to the second edition specifically to this individual "reader" and not to "readers."

The novel, says Ayala, like its more respected sister philosophy, offers spiritual direction to fill the void left by the breakdown of the dogmatic system of beliefs which before the Renaissance provided Christians with a congruous and dependable explanation of the world. Sartre uses literature to illustrate or incarnate his philosophical system, but the Spanish existentialist Unamuno resists systemizing his philosophical thought, preferring the novel as a vehicle for discovering and interpreting reality, not for illustrating it. He is opposed to the concept of Zola's experimental novel because it makes science of literature and studies man as a thing. For Unamuno, novels are read to seek answers to eternal questions and the author's personal—and in no way authoritative—answers are considered by the reader, who then offers his own.

Ayala traces the influence of Cervantes and Galdós in Unamuno, citing his *San Manuel Bueno, Mártir (Good Saint Manuel, Martyr)* as the culmination of the latter's creation, achieving "that elegance which only economy confers."[5] He sees as Unamuno's chief originality his use of the novel not to express something, but to express himself, equating the novel with life itself by integrating imaginary and practical reality. Ayala cannot quite accept, however, Unamuno's elimination of setting, which reduces his characters to bare nuclei of personality—envy, maternity, egocentrism—resulting in an insufferable intensity which enervates the reader and deprives the author of subtle emotional variations.

Unamuno's method of creating *a lo que salga* (however it comes out) sometimes produces unfortunate results, revealing an obvious disdain toward art and excessive sarcasm. While Unamuno's fictionalization of himself in his novels is of Cervantine inspiration, he does not allow a distance between author and alter ego. He does not include humor either since for him reason belongs to the realm of comedy and comedy is completely useless. Comedy is dedication to "unimportant" trivial things which divert us from the consciousness of death, and is therefore tragic. Ayala objects by stating that life is made up of both transcendental and trivial elements; thus, if the novel is to interpret the sense of life, it must contain both and be "tragicomedy." Unamuno shows no liking for things or indulgence for man, and bereft of humor, his novels open onto the perspective of death, producing vertigo. Ayala is reluctant to call this a flaw because the "novel is a genre which each author must adapt to his own expressive needs to abstract and transmit in an original way his own vision of the world," something Unamuno certainly did.[6] We might say that he was original to a fault.

From our author's impressions of Unamuno, consequences for his own writings may be perceived. He admires Unamuno's individualism but misses humor and circumstance which are in accord with his own preferences. It is interesting to note that Ayala sees some limitations imposed on the novel by its very nature which is to interpret human life, even though an author may choose to elude direct human reference by the use of animal characters. Since life implies tension in time, the novel may distort time but cannot eliminate the impression of the unfolding of events in a temporal context. Since chronological alteration is so much a part of our novelist's creation, this enunciation represents a significant limitation on how far time may theoretically be tampered with.

In conclusion, it is possible to see a contrast between Unamuno and Galdós somewhat analogous to Quevedo and Cervantes. While Ayala evidently admires all four as novelists, his own work is more in line with Cervantes and Galdós who show indulgence and compassion toward their creatures whereas Quevedo and Unamuno, each in his own peculiar way, are exceptionally fine writers whose humor takes the form of sarcasm or satire, and whose work reveals their impatience with humanity.

III   Related Topics: Translation and Cinema

In his *Problemas de la traducción* (*Problems of Translation*), Ayala suggests as the primordial prerequisite to a successful translation that the translator be a writer, and that he have sufficient spirit of abnegation to use his writing talent to promote someone else's work and perhaps even accept blame for its faults. Analyzing the two alternatives of literal translation or free adaptation, he finds neither completely satisfactory, advising that each case be treated separately, for a scientific or philosophical work requires more literal translation while adaptation facilitates the transmission of aesthetic values. The sensitivity and intuition of a talented writer must come into play in order to render accurate and artistic translations of literary creations. The essayist considers translation an unattainable ideal since something will inevitably be lost in trying to communicate in another language the complex verbal structure of a work of art which involves a cultural and social system as well as the individual author's expression. Ayala's own work in what he considers a very important yet thankless task includes twelve volumes of translations, ranging from Thomas Mann fictions to discursive works dealing with sociology and literary theory.[7]

The first of our author's essays on the cinema is dated 1929 and the most recent, 1965, showing his continuing interest in the theme. Besides dealing with sociological considerations such as the influence of commercial and governmental interests, he examines the compensatory function of movies in providing the masses with satisfaction for their imaginative needs. Ayala's essay on "Histrionismo y representación" ("Histrionics and Acting") is directed more specifically toward investigating the nature of comedy. In the deliberate fiction of combining the noble and the abject, he sees a source of real life humor produced by inconsistencies in the public figure as a private man. The type of humor analyzed here, residing in the contrast between public dignity and personal flaws, may be observed in our novelist's creations in the bishop of "The Ailing King" who runs from Mass to relieve himself. The incident on a superficial level may seem simply funny, but it has profound moral implications in the story. Other dignified personages who are made to seem ridiculous are the philosopher Antuña in "A Story by Maupassant" and Captain Ramírez in "The Captain's Beard," but in both cases the humorous aspects of the anecdotes lead us to considerations of man's vulnerability in general as well as our own. As Ayala indicates in his essay on histrionics, humor may awaken our deepest responses and may be a spiritually moving experience, but there is always the risk that the spectator may not go beyond a superficial reaction. In comic actors of great personality such as Charlie Chaplin, and Cantinflas, however, humor can assume metaphysical proportions.

IV *Literary Theory*

Our author's usual approach to literary theory is inductive, that is to say that it is induced by the reading of particular authors or texts. Surprisingly enough, not until 1970, a full forty-five years after publishing his first novel, did Ayala offer a book which is theoretical in its approach: *Reflexiones sobre la estructura narrativa (Reflections on Narrative Structure)*.[8] Although ideas are presented and then illustrated in deductive fashion, many of the examples have been analyzed in previous studies, indicating that these theories were arrived at after many years of inductive analysis.

The importance of this book can hardly be overestimated, for in addition to examples taken from other authors, Ayala refers to his own fictions, so it may be inferred that the theories expounded inform his creative writing to a great extent.

Our critic characterizes literature as an eminently impure and ambiguous art form because it is constructed with words which, unlike musical notes or colors in painting, have varied semantic connotations, so that it is inevitably forced to say things beyond its aesthetic intent. Content cannot be eluded so it is futile to seek "pure poetry," though it may be approached by reducing plot to almost nothing in order to concentrate primarily on the elaboration of language. One of the greatest achievements in this respect is Góngora's *Polifemo (Polyphemus)*, but in general, efforts to eliminate content are unsatisfactory in that they leave us with a sensation of triviality.

Ayala tries to identify the specific qualities of the imaginary work in prose or in verse which he calls "the poem" and its relation to elements of outside reality that may enter into it. He cites the prologue of Juan Alfonso de Baena to his *Cancionero (Anthology)* of the fifteenth century, declaring that the writer of poetry should be in love or should "pretend to be," in order that the fiction may convey sincerity. Our author opposes the criterion that literature presupposes aesthetic intention since all use of language involves conscious or unconscious elaboration to achieve maximum effectiveness. Even a piece intended for practical purposes, such as Cicero's speeches designed to thwart Catiline, may be of exceptional artistic merit. The original context is virtually unimportant for the present-day reader, for whom the Cicero speech functions as if it were a work of fiction. "What makes a text a work of literary art . . . is that the imaginative projection of its content produces a configuration of language in which aesthetic value is incorporated."[9] The artistic quality confers on it a certain autonomy which separates it from the particular historical circumstances which might have inspired the work and preserves it from the passing of time.

"The poem" is a self-contained structure. Its art lies not in imitation of nature, but in creative reproduction within the sphere of the imagination, and is not dependent upon plot since the same basic plot may produce very different works in different or even the same authors. "The plot is not the poem, although the poem cannot eliminate plot."[10]

One of the "dynamic centers" of literature is the author and his relation to the work. The poem is nourished by his practical experience, and it is immaterial whether this experience be rooted in direct involvement, dreams, or reading. There is a tendency for the reader to take the convention of fiction for reality, an impression which is enhanced by the use of first-person narrative. Even when the writer works with true events, as soon as he projects them onto an imaginary plane, he changes from subject or witness to a fictionalized character (that is, narrator or actor). The imaginative work absorbs, assimilates, and incorporates its author as an essential element of its structure so that the supposed reality or fantasy of the experience upon which it is based is irrelevant. The author may disguise his presence in a pseudonym, a purely impersonal narrator, several different narrators, characters, or a prologue.

Another phenomenon which interests Ayala and evokes concepts which represent a great contribution to literary study is the role of the reader, both outside the frame of the poem and fictionalized within its structure. The author presupposes an eventual reader who belongs to the structure of the work in that he influences its configuration. The reader may not coincide with the author's originally intended audience just as the Roman senators to whom Cicero directed his speeches are no longer the readers of today. This phenomenon is also true in the case of letters read as works of art which were directed to specific individuals. The reader imagined by the author may not coincide at all with the reader outside the frame of the poem just as our vision of the author, deduced from material within the poem, may have little correspondence to the author as a human being situated outside his creation. The literary experience is based on a convention: the author purports to tell the truth and the reader pretends to accept it as such, and there is no requirement that either the author or reader be portrayed as each is in objective reality within the confines of the self-contained novelistic structure.

Ayala examines several means by which the author makes his supposed reader appear installed within his creation: for example, in prologues characterizing him as dear, curious, or discreet reader, or in characters who function as audience. In the prologue of *Lazarillo de Tormes*, the reader is apt to associate himself with the personage to whom Lázaro addresses himself. Sometimes authors seem to confide in their readers above their characters' heads, establishing an intimate rapport which draws the readers into the texture of the work.

In these *Reflections on Narrative Structure*, Ayala comes to terms with a much discussed literary problem of our times—that of *engagement* or commitment. In his opinion, if the author wishes to express a thesis in his work it must be kept subordinate because if it is aggressive and imposing its violence destroys the harmony of the structure which rests on a delicate balance. Concrete, time-oriented content experiences aesthetic "transubstantiation" only when it is projected toward poetic fiction and is completely integrated within its structure where it becomes less dependent on time. The value of truth is extraneous to aesthetic value, which emanates from complex verbal structures so that great literary works may emerge from content which is unoriginal or even unacceptable (in the religious, political, or philosophical order).

Great writers have the capacity to stimulate eventual readers to confront the mysteries of the universe and their own conscience that reflects these mysteries. Literature involves the transmission of intuitions intended to awaken analogous intuitions in the reader. This is literature's supreme moment. It must be acknowledged, however, that the poem does not produce identical reactions in all readers in all times. Pretensions to eternity therefore are futile since art is subject to historical mutations and changes implicit in the evolution of language itself. It does, nevertheless, endure longer than individual experience. Its success as an artistic creation is not to be found in the materials of experience used nor in formal artifice, but in the author's infusion of his own untransferable intuitions which give form to these elements.

The novel is for Ayala the maximum achievement of narrative literature of which the story and news report are primary forms. The novel, in contrast to these forms concerned principally with anecdote and situation, changes the center of gravity toward concrete human life seen as a process, imitating the open sequence of life itself. The *Lazarillo* provides the opportunity to observe the transformation of story into novel according to the criteria our author offers.

That these are not just theoretical lucubrations is clearly evidenced in the extent to which Ayala's work incorporates his ideas. His special interest in the fictionalization of the author is demonstrated in his insistent use of the first-person narrative as a quick inventory of his fictions reveals. All of the following works contain at least one narrator who is to varying degrees a fictional representation of the author: *Tragicomedy of a Man Without a Spirit;* "Dead Hour"; the prologue of *The Usurpers* and two of its stories: "San Juan de Dios" and "The Bewitched"; the proem and four out of five stories of *The Lamb's Head;* in *Monkey Story,* the title story, "The Captain's Beard," "A Story by Maupassant" and "The Unknown Colleague"; *Dog's Death; The Bottom of the Glass;* the introduction to *The Abduction;* and the story, "A Fish." His *Garden of Delights,* discussed in the next chapter, includes no less than twenty-five narrators. First-person narration is scarce in the vanguard fictions in which the intense elaboration of imagery tends to set a distance between the reader and the story to permit intellectual consideration and aesthetic appreciation from afar without the obvious presence of the author. Four stories of *The Ace of Clubs* also relegate the narrator to a position of marginality and anonymity which is unusual in our author's imaginative works. The creation of some fifty different "I's" corroborates the fact that he is especially fond of fictionalizing himself in such a way that it is impossible to recognize among these many alter egos the "real" Francisco Ayala who exists outside of his fictions.

Equally interesting are the multiple roles assigned to the reader within our novelist's works. We find ourselves the narrator's confidant in "Monkey Story," eavesdroppers on characters' inner thoughts in "The Captain's Beard" and in the last section of *The Bottom of the Glass*, and future readers who form "posterity" for Pinedo in *Dog's Death*. We also become the public as readers of newspapers in *The Bottom of the Glass*, and finally, in Ayala's later works, *The Garden of Delights* and subsequent narratives, we assume numerous other roles which invite our participation in a variety of unusual ways.

CHAPTER 11

Narrative Innovation

E *l jardín de las delicias (The Garden of Delights)*, 1971, and subsequent narrative works are marked by a special interest in the exploration of new modes of narrative expression. In this chapter we will examine innovative procedures such as the incorporation of pictorial art and the use of diverse narrative forms such as newspaper reports, dialogues, and vignettes. Ayala's most recent writings exploit the closeness between "experience and invention," as he titled a book of essays in 1960, in personal anecdotes or observations which, while not fictitious, appear to be so, proving the old adage that truth is stranger than fiction. These latest creations represent a nexus between novel and essay, a blending of genres in a middle ground which constitutes an exciting literary discovery.

The Garden of Delights, which was awarded the prestigious *Premio de la Crítica* (Critics' Prize) of 1972 in Spain, is a masterfully conceived mosaic which is as powerful in its total effect as in each of its parts. From its extraordinary book jacket, illustrated with paintings of Bosch to its moving and enigmatic epilogue, it is a work which brings us before the question of the very essence of literary creation as a personal and universal experience.

I *Fiction, Painting, and Sculpture*

The paintings reproduced on the jacket of *The Garden of Delights* are two doors of Bosch's triptych of the same title. As a prelude to the contrasting visions of the world in the book's content, the first panel is a nightmarish and hallucinatory scene of people, animals, and objects while the other is an equally strange but peaceful rendering of Christ, the first couple, and the flora and fauna of Eden. The paintings are complemented by two quotes referring to Bosch and his visions: "Bosch didn't paint pictures so strange as what I saw," by Quevedo, and "Oh, how well Bosch painted! Now I understand his fancy. You will see incredible things," by Gracián. We can see then that these and the sixteen other illustrations of painting and sculpture which appear in the book serve the same function as Ayala's frequent use of literary allusions: to add to his inventions a dimension of universality and timelessness. The artistic creations of others live for us as vital experiences incorporated in our own sphere of life. In the title of Ayala's story "Angel of Bernini, My Angel," the famous statue of the Pont Sant'Angelo in Rome, photographed in the text, is incarnated in a particular woman of personal significance to the narrator.

Ayala shows us by means of the pictorial illustrations how great works of art are transmuted into elements of fiction. In *"Au cochon de lait"* ("The Suckling Pig"), the narrator sees the Springtime painted by Botticelli enter a restaurant, accompanied by Mercury and a little angel, exactly as in the picture reproduced in the book. In other selections figures in "Samson Killing the Lion" by Dürer, "San Jerónimo" by Alonso Cano, Picasso's "Minotaur and Sleeping Woman," "Nymphs and Satyrs" by Rubens, and figures of Titian's "Sacred and Profane Love" become characters of Ayala's fictions. It seems as justified to consider these as literary illustrations of the paintings and sculptures as it is to say that the latter serve as illustrations of the fictions. On another level, they hark back to the emblematic art of the Renaissance.

II *The Daily Press, Mirror of Our World*

The first section of *The Garden of Delights*, corresponding to the first panel of Bosch's triptych, bears the title of the nineteenth-century Spanish romantic author José Espronceda's *Diablo mundo (Devil's World)*, and consists of ten "Clippings from Yesterday's Daily *News*" and seven "Dialogues of Love" which leave us with the same impression as the pun in a citation from Gracián which precedes: that *mundo* (world) is better expressed as *inmundo* (filthy).

A sort of introduction to the fictitious news items is a report from a Parisian newspaper of 1921 about a train robbery and subsequent execution of a young accomplice Mécislas Charrier whose story was told by the famous French writer André Salmon in his *Souvenirs sans fin (Endless Memories)*. The woman who had been the lover of Salmon's friend Mécislas Golberg and mother of Charrier had aban-

doned the baby who was reared by his father in a hovel only to die
an ignominious death. Why, asks the author, does he recall this long
forgotten and not particularly unusual true incident? "Perhaps
because, for some time now, I have been creating false news stories
which essentially are all too real, attempting to use the daily press as
a mirror of the world we live in and compendium of life, whose
grotesque futility is written in the tachygraphy of that disastrous
fate."[1]

Helplessness and futility form the subsoil of the news stories
which follow, punctuated with the ironic contrast of macabre
humor. Some reveal the perversion of "universal" values such as
love, motherhood, and heroism. There is the case of the starlet *Du-
quesa Luna* (Moon Dutchess) whose death from an overdose of bar-
bituates brings under suspicion her "friend" and "protector"
Inocencio Caballero whose name is ironic since he is neither innocent nor a gentleman. When a note is found expressing her
desperate love for her pimp, the latter is exonerated from all responsibility which is outrageous in view of the whole social situation it
represents. All this is treated with exaggerated delicacy in official
news language. Even more abominable is the item entitled "To
Please Lover, Mother Kills Her Little Daughter," illustrating the
"ferocity of the human condition" confirmed all too often in real
news stories about child abuse and infanticide. Other examples
show the extremes of overcrowdedness which in Japan force a
married couple to seek the privacy of a public park in order to make
love, and of solitude as in the case of the garbage-picker Virtudes
Sola (meaning Virtue Alone) who is "Another Millionaire Beggar."
Then there is the schoolteacher whose avarice expresses itself in the
extreme atrocity of denying food to his only daughter (thirty-seven
years old!) and to himself while the psychiatrists "are not inclined
to certify that his mental health is deficient" (26). He is appropriately named Mendieta—a play on *mendigo* (beggar) and *en
dieta* (on a diet). This case is included in the story of Virtudes Sola
as a previously reported incident.

In "Isabelo Says Good-by," hysterical teenagers surround the
plane of their departing idol Isabelo whose name reveals his
effeminate nature. The loquacity of the news reporter contrasts with
the "uf" and gestures of the girl he interviews whose inability to express herself suggests that she has not only been "bewitched," but
has assumed a virtually subhuman state because of such fervent
adoration. "Science and Industry: New Product" describes the ul-

timate advance of science in the perfection of a Japanese model of a woman, Akiko Plura, which is an improvement over the inflatable Frau Ersatz who relieved the tensions of the German Army in the Second World War, and of the American Rubber Dance Partner, also known as Mr. Mongo. According to the report, self-service installations are envisioned in the United States. The news writer of "Cultural Activities: A Notable Lecture" describes with condescending humor and lyrical tangents the lecture delivered by Dr. Nocedal Cascales (suggesting *nueces cascadas* or "jaded nuts") about the biology of old age. His refutation of the false notion of waning sexual capacity in the older human male is received with great enthusiasm by his elderly audience and is proved, according to the famous poet Jiménez Mantecón (who Rosario Hiriart identifies as Juan Ramón Jiménez Mantecón[2]), by his actual presence.

"Un *quid pro quo* or Who Is Who" is a macabre but humorous report of mistaken identity which occurs when two stewardesses have an auto accident and one is killed and the other hospitalized. Due to a mix-up in documents, the parents of the dead girl visit the bandaged girl in the hospital while the mother of the girl who was hospitalized accepts the corpse as that of her daughter. She does this because she assumes that the mortician has rendered her daughter as unrecognizable as a beautician in a stewardess school once did. The name of the dead girl—Linda (Beautiful)—seems to justify this understandable confusion.

"Otra vez los gamberros" ("The Hoodlums Again") reports a senseless attack on an old man who was walking in the "Park of the Heroes" with his eight-year-old grandson. The reader's indignation is aroused because the police were called by someone who did not dare to intervene while the child was drowned in the "delightful pool" of the park when he tried to bite one of the teenagers, whose names, of course, are withheld because they are minors. The fact that the perpetrators are still laughing about their "joke" is atrocious.

The news section concludes with two letters to the editor. In the first, a retired gentleman whose only occupation is feeding the pigeons complains about the city's compaign to eradicate them. He signs his letter Genaro (for *enero,* January) Frías (cold) Avendaño (for *ave,* bird, and *daño,* harm). The other letter cites the deficient cleaning of streets dirtied by "hundreds of dogs" and at the same time complains about traffic, subways, airplanes, and the noise of radios and televisions. "Certainly one becomes accustomed to everything, but there is a limit" (42), concludes Eufemia de Mier whose name may be creatively translated as Euphemistic Lifshitz.[3]

A curious and perhaps significant coincidence may be noted in that the surname Martín is repeated in four characters: the grandfather and child assaulted in the park, the mute teenager interviewed at Isabelo's departure, and the mother who hammers her infant to death to please her lover. It seems to indicate that the human family is too often presided over by *Marte* (Mars), the Greek diety of war.

III   *Dialogues of Love*

In the second part of the "Devil's World" section of *The Garden of Delights,* Ayala renews his interest in the dialogue which he used previously in a scene of his early novel *Tale of a Dawn* and in the "Dialogue of the Dead" in *The Usurpers.* By completely eliminating the narrator's role, the dialogue form is capable of transmitting experiences with untempered directness and immediacy as if they were taking place right before us. The title "Dialogues of Love" is somewhat explained by the reproduction of the title page of León Hebreo's *Dialoghi di Amore* in the princeps of 1545, but instead of pleasant Neoplatonic dialogues about the theoretical nature of love, we are confronted by dialogues that illustrate the debasement of love in a "devil's world."

The "Diálogo entre el amor y un viejo" ("Dialogue Between Love and an Old Man") reproduces part of Ayala's letter which accompanied the piece when it was sent to Camilo José Cela for his journal *Papeles de Son Armadans.* There he calls his dialogue a *quisicosa* or puzzler which clever readers may find autobiographical or discover to be an "indecent plagiarism," depending on their knowledge of Rodrigo Cota. The allusion to this fifteenth-century convert of Toledo, author of a "Diálogo entre el Amor y un viejo," identifies our author's dialogue as a reworking of this piece, and at the same time serves as a warning to those who too easily see autobiographical implications in what they read.

In Ayala's "Dialogue" a young woman provokes an evasive old man to respond to her advances only to laugh at him and win a bet with her girl friend. Cota's dialogue, in medieval fashion, presents a didactic allegory in which an abstract allegorical figure of Love incites a retired old man to embrace her and then calls his attention to his physical decay, leaving him duly chastised. Our author's version, more fast moving—like our modern times—replaces the didactic-expository tone of the original with more playful, mischievous, and seductive language. While it preserves much of the animal imagery and content of Cota's piece, Ayala's dialogue incorporates numerous other literary allusions such as Apuleius's *Golden Ass* and Shakespeare's *Midsummer-Night's Dream,* both suggestive of asinine behavior. The implications are very different from those of the model since at the end the old man harbors some hope that the "enchanting creature" will return. This conclusion stresses the all too human vulnerability of an old man exposed to ridicule for trying to recuperate a tender flower from the Garden of Eden.

"*Un ballo in maschera,*" whose Italian title recalls Verdi's famous opera of 1859, presents various anonymous voices with vertiginous leaps from one conversation to another in a masquerade. An "ingenious" disguise captures the essence of our confused times: a figure wearing a mask on the back of its head and the clothes backwards so that it appears to be going in the wrong direction. A distorted view of the scene is presented from the perspective of a drunk who laughs at the pomp and vanity of the world as he observes from the floor the horrible foot of an old lady. One voice confides that she has just sneaked away from a funeral; another admonishes an overprotected chubby son, all dressed in white, to drink his milk. In a heavily charged atmosphere of trysts, insults, bad odors, and homosexual conversations, we finally hear a cry to the overprotective mother that her son is being attacked in the telephone booth. This remark is followed by the comment: "It's a scandal! They're going to burst the booth" (56) which expresses a concern not for the abused victim but rather for the telephone booth. The setting of the dialogue bears some resemblance to Mariano José de Larra's famous article "El mundo todo es máscaras" ("All the World Is Masked") which also presents a negative view of society in 1833.

"The Party's Over," whose title reflects a famous song of the fifties, is the dialogue of a couple cleaning up "a ton of filth" after a party as they discuss some of their guests: Teretas, "a pig"; Suspirante (meaning "sighing") an obnoxious homosexual, and rich old Don Tolete (*tolete* is slang for "dollar") who is married to a young girl. The question at the end: "Should we take the trash out now?" is ludicrous, since it is obvious that the trash went out when the guests left.

"Himeneo" ("Hymenean") presents the dialogue of a mother

consoling her daughter who is about to marry an old man who fawns over her (perhaps a previous view of Don Tolete from "The Party's Over"). The mother's insults and analogies ("It's like getting a vaccination" and "no worse than having a tooth pulled") are of little avail in this situation so often appearing in Spanish literature of the Golden Age.

In "*Memento mori*," a woman confides in a neighbor or friend her desperation because her husband, sent home from the hospital with an incurable illness, neither improves nor dies. Her insistence that her own suffering is much worse than that of the dying man reveals her egotism and impatience to free herself from the burden. One wonders whether marriage or life itself is the incurable illness which serves as a reminder of death.

"Exequias por *Fifí*" ("Exeques for *Fifí*") is a revealing title since the adjective *fifí* in Spanish indicates "queer," being also a pun on a dog's name which better describes the masters. The latter, "mama" and "papa" of the deceased animal who was treated as a daughter, lament her passing and berate each other for their conduct toward her. Their lament, recalling Pleberio's famous *planto* over the body of his daughter Melibea at the end of Fernando de Rojas's *Celestina*, and their comment: "Thus pass the glories of the world" contrast grotesquely with the canine condition of the deceased. At first the reader wonders whether there are some erratas in the text as the "papa" uses the masculine form of adjectives when addressing the "mama" who uses feminine forms in self-reference. Gradually, however, it becomes clear that in this homosexual "marriage" the beloved Fifi was a motive of jealousy. Paradoxically, the masters, raising Fifi to their own level by considering her a real daughter, have lowered themselves to an animal or perhaps sub-animal level, inasmuch as the dog looked down on her owners.

The next dialogue, "*Gaudeamus*," is even more shocking. Named after the drinking songs of medieval students, the dialogue presents a dissolute "Student-Poet" leading a young girl into a veritable "cave of ogres," rampant with bad odors, drinking, and sex. An announcer (a devil?) welcomes them to the "Learned Academy," warning against the temptations of the world, the devil, and the flesh. The dialogue creates a scene which could not possibly be presented visually without being very offensive, but the dialogue cannot be considered pornographic since its effect is eased by metaphorical circumlocutions and its obvious purpose is to awaken the reader's indignation toward this type of conduct. The announcer is the spokesman for this "Learned Academy" of vice, calling our attention to the "edifying scene." Euphemistic allusions to maternity, religion, and classical culture accentuate the prostitution of these traditional values. The absence of a narrator is especially important here since it represents the refusal of the author-narrator to dirty his hands in this scene corresponding to the illustration of Rubens's painting of "Nymphs and Satyrs." If Ayala's story "The Ace of Clubs" involved erotic hedonism in private, "*Gaudeamus*" is even more distressing since here it is public and collective.

The title evokes the well-known drinking song "*Gaudeamos igitur*" from Romberg's lovely operetta *The Student Prince* which was produced in 1924 and depicts a nostalgic romance of young love in old Heidelberg in an untroubled world. (The song also forms part of Brahms's *Academic Festival Overture*.) All the tenderness of the operetta is opposed by the debauchery of the Student-Poet of Ayala's dialogue which marks the fall of a student and a poet, and perhaps that of a whole generation for which *gaudeamus* (let's have fun) has become a motto.

IV Lyrical Narrative

"Días felices" ("Happy Days"), the second part of *The Garden of Delights*, consists of literary vignettes narrated in the first person with a lyrical, personal tone giving the impression that the narrator is the author himself which, dealing with fiction, is not at all a reliable impression. All were written in the 1960's with the exception of "Día de duelo" ("Day of Mourning") dated 1941. The pieces are arranged in chronological order of human development—childhood, maturity, and old age—rather than in the order in which they were written.

The title "Happy Days" is ironic in that happiness appears inevitably linked to sorrow because, like the Garden of Delights, it is ephemeral, and its recollection leaves a bittersweet echo of words repeated several times in Ayala's fictions: *Sic transit gloria mundi.* In some selections, experiences long since past are recalled while in others, the narrator describes the present. In the seemingly trivial experiences recounted in these stories, supernatural forces of angels, divine messengers, amulets, and enchanted gardens oppose witches, spells, the menace of time, forgetfulness, and finally death.

The first four stories revive episodes from the narrator's childhood, incidents that probably passed unnoticed by others, but which for the child were traumatic. "A las puertas del Edén" ("At the Doors of Eden") recalls the child's delight at finding a smooth "magic" piece of wood upon which his mother copied a lovely bird which he later found scratched with a nail. He knew it would never recover its original beauty even though his mother promised to repair it. The story insinuates the culpability of the child's brother, and, evoking the Cain motif, reiterates the definitive expulsion from Eden, for his mother stopped painting as other children and obligations came. The child's anguished cry: "Mama, mama, mama!" is much more than a lament for a ruined possession; it is the first cry of pain at finding himself alone and helpless before the closed doors of his childhood paradise.

In "Lección ejemplar" ("Exemplary Lesson"), the narrator remembers having been brought to witness the whipping which Captain Santiago Zegrí received from his mother for having sent her as a souvenir of the wars in Morocco, a box containing five heads of Moors he had killed. When the narrator asks why not seven or eight heads, he alludes to the famous Spanish epic poem *The Seven Infantes of Lara* in which a similar scene occurs. The Captain's name Santiago is that of the Apostle Saint James, patron saint of the Christians in their seven centuries of war against the Moors in Spain which ended in 1492, but his surname Zegrí is a fairly common one of Moorish origin. This underscores the irony of his enmity toward the Moors suggestive of José Torres's situation in *The Lamb's Head* upon discovering Moorish relatives. Not only is there an exemplary lesson for the young protagonist who cannot forget the Captain's punishment, but also, as the allusions to history, legend, and this century's war in Morocco show, a lesson for Spain.

The narrator of "Nuestro jardín" ("Our Garden") yearns to recover the paradisiacal family garden of the picture his mother had painted before he was born. "Everything disappears," his mother warns, and when they finally pass near the garden, it is hidden from view behind a high wall. The reader realizes that this garden is "our garden" too (the first person plural is intentional), a faraway legend never to be recuperated.

"Día de duelo" ("Day of Mourning") is described by the narrator in the midst of the oppression he feels before the rigid body, evidently that of his father, which "like an abandoned mask" has turned the games of hide-and-seek he played with his children into a sad reality. His whole life, then, was a deception, and now the narrator and his brothers distrust one another: "Who could trust anyone after your running away?" Addressing himself to the dead man, the narrator expresses poignantly the discovery of death which for him means a loved one's hiding and leaving only a false mask discarded and a grieving son who realizes his own fraudulent existence.

A rush of adjectives and a torrent of phrases precipitate the reader into the recalled festivities of "San Silvestre" ("Saint Sylvester")—a certain New Year's Eve the narrator and other "young, impatient, avid Spaniards" spent in a rathskeller in Germany. Accompanied by their mentor, a picturesque personage named the Marquis of Saint Denis (perhaps for Dionysos, the deity of drink), they drink and dance around the trademark symbol of Bockbeer—a papier mâché billy goat. The narrator is beckoned by a mother-daughter team and joins them, feeling attracted to both. Suddenly he finds himself on the floor surrounded by some laughing old cleaning women "armed with brooms" before the billy goat which, as at a witches' sabbath, presides.

Another selection reproducing an experience of a young man is "Postrimerías" ("The Triumph of Death"), referring to a famous painting by Valdés Leal which the narrator and his fiancée admire in the Hospital of Charity. The narrator recalls verses of Mira de Amescua: "Tomb of bones covered / with a cloth of brocade" and then they look at Murillo's painting of Saint Elizabeth of Hungary curing lepers with her queenlike hands. After a walk through the beautiful hospital patio, certain events appear to suggest the subjects of these art works. The girl pets a mangy, lame dog which the narrator views with distrust, seeing in the lameness and glowing eyes a malignant presence. His companion insists on consoling the animal, even though it will no doubt suffer "later." The narrator now repeats: "Lord, what happy days! But later . . . "(115).

For the mature narrator of "El ángel de Bernini, mi ángel" ("Angel of Bernini, My Angel"), the sculptor of the famous statue of the Sant'Angelo Bridge in Rome anticipated its human encarnation in the woman he loves. Because of their separation, he suffers knowing that he will see the statue and never again be able to touch its human model. Man can only understand the Divine in terms of his own profane experience, Ayala seems to indicate, as the narrator remembers that he gave her a cross to recall their "passion," and she promised to kiss it each night while praying to her guardian angel.

The narrator of "¡Aleluya, hermano!" ("Hallelujah, Brother") finds himself depressed by personal problems, above all that of "killing time" on a long lonesome Sunday. An older man befriends him, invites him to his humble home, and plays the clarinet for him. The music, like a song of life itself, goes from playful to lamenting tones, then to silence, melancholy quiet, and a closing cry of jubilation as the old man calls out "Hallelujah, brother," and the narrator is ready to go back into the dance of life.

"Entre el *grand guignol* y el *vaudeville*" ("Between the *Grand Guignol* and *Vaudeville*") is the story of an adultery to which the narrator is part, but nonetheless seems amazed by the complacency of his lover as she manages to elude the electronic surveillance of her scientist husband. The irony of the situation is enhanced by allusions to popular songs like "The Magic of Your Smile," "Black Magic," and by literary references. Like Poe's raven, the woman makes a false promise of "Never more" to her husband, and "Poe's letter" becomes the lovers' password because like the purloined letter ingeniously hidden in an obvious place, they "hide" in the middle of busy Times Square. It is noteworthy that the woman surpasses both her scientist husband and her lover in perversity and ingenuity.

In "*Au cochon de lait*," ("The Suckling Pig") the narrator recalls a waiter who years before in the same restaurant recited stanzas of the *Divine Comedy* while outside in the streets the *Comédie humaine* (human comedy) took place. The rest of the story involves a similar contrast between the divine and the profane. When a family of three enters the restaurant the narrator sees in the flesh Botticelli's painting of Spring composed of the lovely goddess, a plump young angel, and her gallant husband, Mercury. Their arrival is parodied by that of the meal: a roast pig whose little ears, mouth, and teeth are pointed out by Spring to her little angel. "We too eat *cochon de lait*," adds the narrator, and the reader, now included in that first-person plural, feels the same repulsion as before the monkey feast in "Monkey Story" and the meal in "The Lamb's Head." It seems that spiritual elevation is difficult to sustain, for, as we have seen in Ayala's novels, the body will have its due.

"Fragancia de jazmines" ("Fragrance of Jasmines"), subtitled "Tribute to Espronceda," is a tender rendering of the themes of love, time, and age found in the latter's *Devil's World*, particularly in the second canto, "To Teresa." In addition to reproducing these themes, Ayala incorporates almost imperceptibly whole verses from Espronceda's poem in the text of his story. A mirror and a song, the bolero of the title, evoke in the narrator thoughts of his aging and memories of his great love affair five years before with a young married woman. Her description coincides with that of Teresa in Espronceda's poem who had run away with the poet in a stormy relationship which ended sadly and made him feel old at the age of thirty. Ayala's narrator, however, is no longer a young man and convinces the woman that not only social scandal menaced their love, but much worse, the threat of age and his waning vigor which would inevitably lead to unhappiness. So, in contrast to Espronceda's "sad memories of pleasure past," a difficult "amputation" successfully avoided the "gangrene of the years" leaving sweet and melancholy memories which linger on like the fragrance of very ephemeral flowers. The first-person narration, which permits us to perceive the authentic nostalgia and pain of the narrator's experience, prevents this moving story from falling into the exaggerated sentimentalism so typical of boleros.

As in "The Suckling Pig," a grotesque vision invades the atmosphere of a restaurant in "Magia I" ("Magic I"). As the narrator's friend tells him of the nightmares and fears which torture her love for him, the restaurant suddenly becomes a grotto inhabited by two witches and other horrible creatures. He remembers that as a child he had wanted to disenchant the princess of an Arabian tale changed into a dove just as now he desires to break the spell which torments his love. The effect of the story is intensified by the reproduction of Goya's painting "Two Old Men Eating."

"Magia II" ("Magic II") contains allusions to Baudelaire, Calderón, a French song, a childhood Christmas carol, and a story by Jorge Luis Borges called "Los dos reyes y los dos laberintos" ("The Two Kings and the Two Labyrinths"). The narrator contemplates giving his love a clepsydra of sand as a Christmas gift, but she had accused him of enclosing her in his labyrinth, a desert. With this gift, he feels that his destiny will be inextricably tied to hers, for "the day you forget to invert it, and the sand stops falling, will be my last" (145). Like Borges's story of the two kings and the two labyrinths, two destinies are intertwined, for when she forgets to invert the clepsydra, it will indeed mean that he is no longer remembered. Time leads to forgetfulness and the clepsydra represents a futile effort to seize both time and love and to enclose them forever, for, like the Christmas carol recalled by the narrator, the past cannot be relived.

A number of vignettes transform religious or sacred themes into everyday experience. "En pascua florida" ("At Easter") begins like a poem of circumstance "To Lisa, who has sent an Easter egg she decorated," evoking similar dedications in poems by Garcilaso and Quevedo. The selection begins with words Cervantes used in his poem "Vieje del Parnaso" ("Parnassus Journey") to seemingly belittle his poetic prowess: "If I had the talent heaven denied me. . . ." The narrator subsequently expresses his desire to "perpetuate the ephemeral" (147). He views the decorated egg as a Eucharist, a crystal ball, and symbol of the origin of life representing mystery, the promise of resurrection, or pain and blood. Lisa too is a future promise whose adolescence may awaken pain. Is she the divine messenger of a glorious resurrection or another defenseless creature who will be beseiged by life? The narrator feels himself approaching "the dark threshhold, still questioning, in vain" (147).

Another religious experience is represented in the story "En la Sixtina" ("In the Sistine") which uses the first person plural to associate the reader with the narrator and his companion as they accompany a multitude of people through the galleries leading to the Sistine Chapel. We experience vertigo as the author first directs our eyes up above where Michelangelo's terrible cherubim and Charon direct the Last Judgment, then to the floor where a throng of multilingual tourists circulate, then from hairy legs to bald heads, and finally from feet to braids. "Impenitent sinners" attack the Redeemer with their cameras, and thoughts flow to the spaghetti dinner which awaits them, inspiring Ayala's metaphorical description: "All of us, like a thick mass in a colossal pot, that flows over slowly on one side while the other keeps on filling, went round and round together in the Sistine, round and round, endlessly" (153). The reader feels himself caught up in this immense mixture of the most diverse humanity in a veritable Last Judgment.

A similar theme is repeated in "El Mesías" ("The Messiah") in which the spiritually elevating experience of hearing Händel's great composition is interrupted by the physical discomfort of the hard auditorium seats. "Sad human misery" (160), comments the narrator, noting that the triumphant hallelujah chorus not only transmitted spiritual exultation, but brought with it immense physical relief from the uncomfortable seats. After the "sublime feast" of music, the narrator and his companion consider going to a Chinese restaurant to eat pork, but decide not to. As we have seen in so many Ayala fictions, man's distraction from the nobler elements of life is often the result of his bodily demands.

As if man can only know the Divine by means of the profane, numerous "angels" accompany the narrators of these stories in the form of women. In "El leoncito de barro negro" ("The Little Black Clay Lion"), the narrator awaits the visit of his angel, his "divine messenger whose hands sustain my existence, body and soul," while a black clay lion, a souvenir from Mexico, confronts a picture of his little girl on a tricycle. Like the woman in "Magic II," his "angel" is an enchanted princess transformed by magic into a melancholy dove. By accident, the lion is broken and his angel-lover feels liberated. This motif appears again in "Amor sagrado y amor profano" ("Sacred and profane love"), illustrated by Titian's painting of the same title, in which the narrator, after a long and atrocious struggle, finds himself "in happy possession" of his angel. "Love, a lion/ that devours hearts," he recalls, knowing that his angel, with a smile as ambiguous as that of the statue of the Rheims Cathedral, is capable of expelling him from Paradise. He cannot forget, however, other loves more worldly than this great true love like the "gentle friend" who ministered to him while his "angel" did not, and who left without a scene, saying simply: "Good-by, youth; good-by, love." A magazine advertisement of a woman announcing rum is enough to open the subtle knife wound, showing that each love leaves its mark. Even though the narrator has achieved his great love, another, less transcendental and long since ended, still evokes bittersweet remembrances. Ironically, life with the sublime angel settled into a bourgeoise existence, complete with a glass of whiskey and picture magazine.

"Más sobre ángeles" ("More About Angels") adds another illusory dimension since it seems to comment upon the previously recounted "Angel of Bernini, My Angel." The narrator speaks directly to a woman who "read what I had written about my Angel of Bernini," and wants to know who she is. He tries to convince her that the work of art interests him and not the woman he knew who formed the corporeal reality. His companion's love seems more eternal than the marble of the statue they contemplate, and now she represents for him the "celestial legions of angels" (156).

Three stories are inspired by forms of absence. "Mientras tú duermes" ("While You Sleep"), illustrated by Picasso's "Minotaur and Sleeping Woman," presents the separation wrought by sleep as a simulacrum of death, the ultimate absence. The sleeping presence of the loved one to whom the narrator addresses his thoughts is ironic because she has fled from him to hide in a world of dreams to which he has no access. In "Tu ausencia" ("Your Absence"), introduced by epigraphs of Shakespeare and Baudelaire, the narrator enumerates all the little trivialities of his relationship with his loved one. In her absence, the circle of their "magic embrace" has been broken, and "the outside world which gesticulates, declaims, convulses, full of crimes, social demands, accidents, and programs, is for me only a distant and colorless phantasmagoria" (167). Apparently love is the only refuge from the "devil's world."

"Las golondrinas de antaño" ("The Swallows of Yesteryear") bears as its title a quotation from the Spanish poet Gustavo Adolfo Bécquer, and contains other allusions to famous expressions of nostalgia such as François Villon's "snows of yesteryear," Jorge Manrique's "greenery of the past," and the perennial *ubi sunt* ("where are they?") as the narrator asks: "Where is that restaurant of ours? What happened to it?" (169). In his beloved's absence, the image of "their restaurant," destroyed by fire the year before, provokes desolation despite the prospect of their going together to new places, for it represents part of their lost paradise. What might seem a rather insignificant "tragedy" is elevated to one of life's intimate sorrows by the universality of the literary allusions which frame this vignette.

For the lonely old man who narrates the concluding story, "Música para bien morir" ("Music to Die By"), time hangs heavy, spring holds no promise, and phantoms of the past bring unhappy memories. He turns on the radio as if to grasp a hand in the dark, and the ubiquitous series of "Music for . . . " every occasion obligingly provides him with "Music for the Moment of Death."

One of the most puzzling parts of *The Garden of Delights* is its epilogue in which the author contemplates the diverse pieces of just yesterday and years ago, combined "like the pieces of a broken mirror" which reflect his image. He asks himself why he has sought to preserve in a "coffer of words" love's tortures, fleeting happiness, and the sarcasm implicit in life's delights and pains. Like many of his narrators, the author addresses himself to a woman anticipating with apprehension her reactions in the future, at the end of her days when "those hands that will always be beautiful" open the coffer. But then he concludes that since she is very prudent, she may never dare to lift the cover.

This epilogue, which appears to be almost an extension of the fictional content of the book, leaves the reader perplexed. Its intimate, lyrical tone seems to suggest an autobiographical link, but we are dealing with a literary enigma designed to make it impossible to determine precisely how experience has been transformed into invention.

After the publication of *The Garden of Delights*, Ayala continues to write lyrical prose using the narrative first person, singular and plural, with some notable examples of increased autobiographical suggestion. New in Ayala's fiction, for example, is the statement of an exact date—February 4, 1972—in the setting of "Una mañana en Sicilia" ("One Morning in Sicily") in which the narrator, accompanied by María del Carmen, visits the peaceful amphitheater at Segesta, and then the nearby temple of a long forgotten, now anonymous deity.[4] They see international couples' names carved in thick cactus leaves with past dates, and a wedding party climbing up to the temple with visible fatigue to photograph their moment of happiness before the stone monument. The writer asks himself: "But am I not also consigning this moment of mine to the ephemeral page of a diary?" The melancholy irony makes us feel the futility of the common human aspiration to achieve some measure of eternity, whether it be in cactus leaves, marble, bronze, stone, or paper. As Quevedo said, "all things remind us of death," for the very peacefulness of the ancient amphitheater suggests the final triumph of death.

"This is a dream," insists the narrator of "Un sueño" ("A Dream"), perplexed that everything nevertheless seems so concrete and tangible.[5] Observing a happy Christmas nativity scene, he is suddenly aware of a little angel who covers his eyes. When the angel somehow makes him comprehend that he is crying because he is destined to keep vigil at Christ's tomb, the narrator cites the human practice of rejoicing in happy times and grieving at the time of sorrow, but he himself no longer feels happy. He asks if the angel would prefer that the Divine Child had never come to the world. He is answered by the angel's silence and then he awakes.

As Calderón de la Barca's famous play *La vida es sueño (Life Is a Dream)* demonstrates, Spanish literature has continually dealt with the indistinct quality of dreams and wakefulness. The nativity scene itself underscores this ambiguity, for while it is concrete and made of tangible materials, it is not the "real" nativity scene. Isn't all representation, then, dreamlike, whether it be material or imaginative? Besides treating anew this traditional theme, Ayala's selection brings us to the question of the purpose of life and its happy moments in view of the transitory nature of both.

In "El chalet *art nouveau*" ("The 'New Art' Chalet") the

narrator takes his friend to see first the magnificent cathedral of
Salamanca and then to a nearby chalet he had discovered years
before, already in ruins last year.[6] The chalet is of the same age as
the narrator who keeps an old photograph of it, knowing that next
year its remains probably won't be there any more. As with the
restaurant which evokes nostalgia in "The Swallows of Yesteryear"
in "Happy Days," the chalet is viewed from multiple time perspectives, but here it is identified with the narrator even more closely in
age and style, coinciding with the era of his childhood. Ironically,
the name *art nouveau* or "new art" designates a long dated form
since what is new at one time becomes old with time. As in "One
Morning in Sicily," there is a futile effort to preserve an experience
not only in a photograph, but also in memory, and most important
of all, in sharing it with someone else—the companion to whom the
narrator addresses his thoughts, and by implication, the reader.

"Incidente" ("Incident"), dated October 3, 1975, presents a rare
opportunity to gain insight into Ayala's creative process since it was
published together with the author's own comments in a short essay
entitled "Literary Invention" and was further studied by Rosario
Hiriart in her essay on the "Metamorphosis of an Anecdote."[7] It
begins as a letter written to please a friend from the beach where
the narrator is spending a rather boring vacation. Using the first
person plural, he tells how they had observed with a little uneasiness, a strange, draped, laughing figure of undistinguishable sex
on the next blanket. A little girl stopped to show them some shells
she had found on the beach. Afterwards, alarmed by shouts and an
ambulance siren, they went to investigate, noticing that the sinister
"unisex" figure had disappeared. They hear several unclear versions
of a crime in which a little girl was killed, but the next day the local
newspaper informs that the killer—obviously the strange figure
hidden under a tunic—demented or perhaps on drugs, felt she "had
to kill that day" and knifed a little girl before the eyes of her
horrified mother. While the four-year-old victim lies in a coma, the
incident provides food for conversation in an otherwise uneventful
existence.

The author's explanation contains the following information: the
incident actually occurred while he was vacationing at Fuengirola.
A few days afterward, he felt the desire to give the episode literary
form by selecting and organizing the true materials into a coherent
structure. The pretext of complying with a social obligation dilutes

a particularly atrocious crime by placing it against a background of boredom and triviality. The anonymity of the victim makes the crime seem especially absurd, but the appearance of an actual child is designed to elicit feelings of concern for an individual. Ayala's most interesting revelation, however, is his discovery of profound significance in the story, for his sinister, draped figure with shaven head unwittingly turns out to be a personification of death very much in keeping with its traditional representations, feminine in Spanish by the gender of *la muerte*, and an ominous yet hardly noticed presence often symbolized by a skull. Thus our author realizes what the Surrealists have long recognized as a fact: the value of coincidence and chance in yielding transcendental intuitions.

In her intensive analysis of "Incident" and Ayala's comments, Rosario Hiriart studies several notable aspects such as the attitude of deliberate indifference cultivated in the piece, the explicitly hyena-like appearance of the death figure, the expert handling of pace and suspense, and the multiple time dimensions.[8] Noting in the author's latest "mini-stories" the use of personal anecdotes, the critic includes two short notes given to her by Ayala, dated 1948 and 1949, which show his early interest in giving expression to such incidents. Using personal experiences as a point of departure, "La lucha contra el fascismo" ("The Struggle Against Fascism") shows the irony of indignation against the enemy's atrocities in contrast to pride in one's own equally atrocious acts. In "El ratón y el gato; la paloma y el gavilán" ("The Mouse and the Cat; the Dove and the Hawk") Ayala juxtaposes two seemingly unrelated scenes observed by him (evidently in Argentina): a cat indifferently toying with a mouse and a couple enacting in an Andean dance the pursuit and capture of a dove by a bird of prey. Both scenes impress him as totemic representations of the dangerous situation of police omnipresence and omnipotence which he has been discussing with a friend.

There is, however, an essential difference between these early anecdotes and the more recent "Incident" in that the latter has evidently been subjected to more intensive artistic elaboration in order to give the impression of fiction. While it is unquestionably a narration, as an embellished true story it cannot be categorized peremptorily as fiction, which leads us to consider Ayala's latest experimentation with hybrid genres.

V   *A Strange New Genre*

The culmination of Ayala's innovative attitude toward his craft is his work in developing nonfictional narratives derived from personal involvement or the memoirs, correspondence, and literary works of others which are of timely significance. His characteristic use of traditional plots and literary allusions in his fictions now expands to include whole excerpts of fascinating anecdotes combined with such discursive materials as personal opinions, literary criticism, and even comments on his own work. The result is a unique combination of essay, story, autobiography, and literary extracts presented in a decidedly narrative form, and like hybrid strains of plants, this genre promises to be very fruitful.

Our author, it will be remembered, has warned us time and again in his essays about the dangers of taking the narrator for the author. In his 1975 essay "Thomas Mann en varios tiempos" ("Thomas Mann in Different Times"), he reiterates Plato's statement that poets are liars and explains that fiction, with its reticence and irony, is deceiving, for the success of fiction paradoxically is in taking it for what it is not: the truth.[9] In these new writings, however, it is precisely the concept of fiction itself which is under perusal, demonstrating that narrative literature does not necessarily have to be fictitious.

The transition is most easily observed in "Lake Michigan" which at first seems to correspond to the vein of Ayala's "Happy Days" with its first-person narrative, lyricism and preoccupation with the fugacity of time.[10] This time the narrator's melancholy thoughts are inspired by the sinking of a house on Lake Michigan which evokes the threat posed to Venice by the sea. Recalling the record of "Lake Michigan" he listened to in "the remote Madrid" of his youth, he ponders the "unforeseeable destiny" that "has led me to this shore that devours houses and returns dead fish." Like "Magic I," there are ominous death visions, but at the same time, unmistakable autobiographical indications are present in the reference to his youth in Madrid, a visit from a girl consulting him about a thesis she is preparing on his novels for the University of Venice, and in a discursive discussion of related readings, including Thomas Mann.

The author situates "Inquisidor y rabino" ("Inquisitor and Rabbi"), mentioned previously in connection with the story "The Inquisitor," "right next to my house, here in New York."[11] There, on the corner of Sixteenth Street and Fifth Avenue, he runs into a rabbi who is, he insists, the Inquisitor Don Fernando Niño de Guevara in the flesh, escaped from El Greco's portrait in the Metropolitan Museum of Art. His observation gives rise to conjecture about the real nature of the prelate. The actual encounter is, of course, true, but the author's imagination relates this reality to art, literature, and his own fictions, and "literature of the imagination" is what we commonly call fiction.

In "Todo el año (literalmente) carnaval" ("Carnival All Year Long [Literally]"), the author discusses the tyranny of fashion and the liberating effect of Carnival "over a quarter of a century ago, when I was busy editing my *Treatise on Sociology.*"[12] "Now, in New York, where I live at present," fashion has disappeared and the most outlandish dress is hardly noticed. This phenomenon, says the author, is a sign of extreme social disintegration. He then considers Halloween, a vestige of Carnival in its function as an enactment of witch-hunt, with the ironical observation that the children's festival is formalized once a year while in the adult world it's Carnival all year long. The selection is basically an essay, but the author's description of the strange beings which roam Manhattan's streets lends a fictional quality to the vision.

"Igualdad ante la ley" ("Equality Before the Law") reads like fiction, and like Ayala's "Rape in California" and "Another Millionaire Beggar," it employs the technique of juxtaposing two unusual anecdotes from which significance may be extracted.[13] The author retells a newspaper report about when the police handcuffed and jailed the automotive king, Henry Ford III, for drunken driving "to compensate for not being able to capture the worst criminals." "But today, March 5, 1975," writes the author, "I read in the paper the report that, here in New York" a poor woman detained for speeding was forced to submit to a rectal and vaginal search, which the police called a "normal procedure." Ayala, ever conscious of life's ironies, concludes that only the most heinous crimes seem to elicit admiration, inhibitory respect, and perhaps the envy of the authorities while minor offenses are dealt with severely. The anecdotes seem unbelievable ("fictitious"), but are true. Nevertheless, the raw materials of truth have been subjected to the same procedures Ayala outlined for the elaboration of "Incident," namely selection and structure, and the impact is equally pronounced.

"Todos los caminos llevan a Roma" ("All Roads Lead to Rome") includes the author's description of a religious procession he noticed on Third Avenue in New York on the way home from the airport, and information about the same appearing in the *New York Times* the following day, October 8, 1973.[14] The object of attention was a march of the faithful to the new locale of New York's first homosexual church, the Beloved Disciple. Ayala quotes the article extensively to inform us about all the details, and then quotes a large section from Lucius Apuleius's *Golden Ass,* a veritable "treasury of usable materials" describing a similar procession of homosexuals and their church of the Great Goddess of Syria. Final reference is made to the Spanish language paper *El Mundo de Hoy* of October 20, 1974, which reports on the progress of the homosexual church and the love feast celebrating the betrothal of the subdeacon and the priest. Our author concludes with the ironical exclamation: "May it be for God's sake." He has drawn on various sources, including personal experience, newspaper reports, and a second century Roman writer to prove various clichés: There is nothing new under the sun, truth is stranger than fiction, and "all roads lead to Rome." The selection responds to the same impulse that inspires Ayala's fictions: to probe the human condition and give expression to our times.

Recalling the Gracián line about the world or *mundo* being filthy or *inmundo* which serves as epigraph to Ayala's "Devil's World," the title of "No hay mundo que lo sea" (literally "No World Really Is So") suggests the same alternative, and is, in fact, a play on the Latin *mundus,* from which the Spanish word *mundo* (world) is derived, and also the word *mondo,* meaning "clean."[15] Thus the title may best be rendered as "No World Really Is Clean."

The selection consists of three parts, the first of which is called "Todos los libros son inmorales" ("All Books Are Immoral"). It begins with a quote from the memoirs of an eighteenth-century writer, Count Alexandre de Tilly, who denounces as obscene the acclaimed novel *Les Liaisons dangereuses (Dangerous Connections),* written by Choderlos de Laclos in 1782. This author had revealed to Tilly that his purpose was to write something "that would still resound when I am gone." Ayala comments that a reader or spectator is prone to project an unconscious vengeance upon the person who shows us a disagreeable vision just as Laclos, a decent family man and father, was vituperated as an immoral monster because what he portrayed in his novel was deemed offensive by some, although its literary value was recognized even by Tilly, and even more importantly, by Baudelaire, author of the titular quote, indicating that all books about humanity must inevitably be immoral. This may be considered as Ayala's own defense against criticism of some "shocking" scenes in his novels, specifically the one to which he refers in the second part of "No World Really Is Clean," called "On the Throne."

Our author explains that the particular scene from his novel *Dog's Death*, in which the dictator Bocanegra entertains visitors from his toilet throne, is rooted in his conviction that "crude and naked power used to be—and still is—an obscenity." Even today's demands for "justice" for diverse interest groups often mask a desire for power. Ayala decries society's passive acceptance of violence and atrocities; his enumeration of these crimes recalls similar events in *Dog's Death*. The bathroom scene which some critics found so offensive in this novel is no more so than the centuries' old *lever* ceremony such as that of the Prince of Gales, described in Tilly's *Memoirs*. Citing other historical precedents, Ayala notes that *Esquire* magazine of August 1972 published a report about a similar custom of Lyndon B. Johnson when he was President of the United States. Ayala then quotes Saint-Simon's denigrating portrait of the Duke of Vendôme's habit of entertaining functionaries and dignitaries from his foul "perforated chair" where the obsequious Alberoni paid him homage in a particularly repulsive way which figuratively has become a "sardonic formula for political success." The combination of literary and historical examples and social comment proves that what seems shocking in fiction is all too often accepted in real life, and perhaps for that very reason it is regarded as offensive.

" Cuál es el sexo de los ángeles?" ("What Is the Sex of the Angels?") evokes in its title a controversy which has intrigued theologians not only in the late Middle Ages, but even today.[16] For Ayala, the theological question serves only as a contrast to his recounting of an incident told by Benvenuto Cellini in his *Life*. Cellini, unable to acquire a "lady of the evening" for a party with friends, convinces his young Spanish aide, named Diego, to accompany him dressed as a woman. Diego is the object of effusive admiration, referred to as an angel by Cellini's friends, but the women discover in a hilarious way that "Pomona" is undeniably a man. Ayala adduces this "borrowed" episode from Cellini's *Life*, which occurred in 1523 after a terrible plague had scourged Rome, to illustrate man's tendency to relax after tremendous disturbances such as wars, revolutions, and plagues. Cellini's entertaining story is at the same time very much in accord with Ayala's own use of profane

angels, practical jokes, and humor in his fictions. Retold by our
author, the original incident is given a new dimension far beyond
that of a funny story as it reveals human nature and the need for
humor.

Ayala's latest works bring us before the very act of literary creation as we witness the raw materials of diverse readings and personal references filtered through the author's own inimitable vision
of life and given artistic expression without submitting to established ideas of truth, fiction, or genres. These new narrative essays
or essay-like narratives, just as Ayala's previous novels and essays,
continue to scrutinize in an artistic way man's condition and
destiny.

Recalling our author's fascinating study of fictionalization of the
reader in *Reflections on Narrative Structure,* some examples from
his latest works yield a wide variety of roles assigned to the reader
by techniques which elicit active if unconscious association with fictitious representations in the text. The newspaper reports of
"Devil's World" place us in the position of the general reading
public while the letters addressed to the editor invite us to identify
ourselves with him. The "Dialogues of Love" situate us as a silent
audience outside but directly confronting the events which unfold
before us. The emphatic "we" in *"The Suckling Pig,"* "In the
Sistine Chapel," and "The Messiah" makes it impossible for the
reader to extract himself from the involvement implied by the first
person plural in experiences which have metaphysical implications.
The narrator of "Hallelujah, Brother" solicits our attention as
listeners with the polite you *(usted)* so we don't feel too familiar,
but in "Fragrance of Jasmines," we are eavesdroppers on the
private thoughts and memories of the narrator, as in other narrations, such as "Your Absence," "While You Sleep," "Magic II,"
and "More About Angels," where the narrator addresses the ab-
sent or remembered lover. We are the recipients of a postcard from
the narrator of "Incident" and the readers of a diary in "One Morning in Sicily." Finally, we approach works like "Inquisitor and Rabbi" and "Equality Before the Law" with the attitude of essay
readers, but we must make some adjustments in our expectations
because of the novelistic nature of the factual experiences recounted
in the text.

CHAPTER 12

Summary and Conclusions

OVER fifty years of creative and discursive writing form the works of Francisco Ayala which have been examined in this volume. Besides his outstanding accomplishments in diverse fields of interest, our author's literary production is marked by consistent creation of the highest quality, offering his particular view of life in generally Hispanic contexts, but with a vision that transcends temporal and geographical limitations. At this point, we should reiterate some of the elements which give his works a clearly defined and identifiable character as well as those which are most variable, and will conclude with some considerations regarding his artistic aims.

I Major Themes

Ayala's essays and literary inventions treat certain sustained themes which lend great unity to his expression in both genres. These themes are, of course, interrelated in that they all involve the question of man's destiny. He examines the passions that come into play in man's conduct toward his fellow man. His fictional characters find themselves situated in a world of values in crisis, troubled by social pressures, the lust for power which curtails freedom, the weight of time and the certainty of death, and by their own human weaknesses. Man's vulnerability is communicated by the practical jokes and deceptions to which his characters often fall victim. Man is also the victim of his physical demands which betray him, sometimes with comic consequences, but the reader senses the author's commiseration with his creatures even though the world around them may seem cruel and insensitive. There is an atmosphere of timelessness in Ayala's fictions, enhanced by his consistent utilization of literary precedents in the form of explicit or veiled allusions to Spanish and universal masterworks or by the reworking of "borrowed" themes previously exploited by authors of past ages. Thus, the novel inevitably acquires novelty in the original configuration of essentially limited plots determined by each author's circumstances, experience, purpose, and style.

II *Characteristics of His Inventions*

As we have seen, Ayala favors the first-person narrative in most of his fictions and he enjoys teasing the reader into suspecting autobiographical implications which may indeed be there. It becomes virtually impossible to determine the degree to which actual experience has been artistically disguised or to find the real "I." The only alternative is to accept the narrator as fictitious, thus allowing the author to protect himself from the probing reader. Many of his narrators tend to be callous or of negative traits, which in itself discourages ready identification with the author.

The stories and novels studied are open-ended in that they are deliberately ambiguous. Like life itself, Ayala's inventions present puzzles and enigmas which cannot be considered fully resolved even after critical analysis.

Other constants in these fictions are the use of negative and occasionally scabrous materials with moral connotations such as frequent animal imagery suggestive of man's degradation in certain situations; the presence of humor, not gratuitous, but rooted rather deeply in irony; and constant allusions to Spanish and universal art, including literature, painting, sculpture, and music.

In Ayala's works, the reader finds himself confused by multiple perspectives of events and by the direction of vision vertiginously up, down, and around, close up and far away. Our author's expert manipulation of point of view is just one facet of his very polished narrative technique. Proper names and word play are vehicles of subtle comments, and it is this attention to detail that makes even the briefest selection extremely dense and open to intensive analysis. It is apparent that for Ayala the creative process involves careful artistic elaboration, in part representing conscious awareness of his craft, but in large measure depending upon sheer natural talent.

III *Diversification and Innovation*

As we noted in the preface to this book, an important characteristic of Ayala's narrative is its variety. In a published conversation with Andrés Amorós, our author expresses his satisfaction at not having "plagiarized" himself, one of the dangers of succumbing to the quantitative demands of literary professionalism.[1] This is easily verified by a review of his varied production of novels, novelettes, short stories, vignettes, dialogues, and news reports. These works range in style from the traditional *Tragicomedy of a Man Without a Spirit* to the vanguard *Hunter at Dawn*, the ironic satire of *Dog's Death*, the direct scenes of "Dialogues of Love," the literary reworking of *The Abduction*, and the nostalgic lyrical evocations of "Happy Days." His fictions include varying degrees of the sublime and the ridiculous, the sacred and profane, the humorous and the horrific. The critics who thought they knew the Ayala of *Dog's Death, The Bottom of the Glass*, and *The Ace of Clubs* as a critical satirist were completely disconcerted by "Happy Days." Even his old friend, H. A. Murena, wrote him from Argentina wondering why he had so many illustrations in *The Garden of Delights*. Ayala's attitude toward his literary creations is one of constant inventiveness and experimentation which in his most recent incursions into the very nature of the transformation of experience into creative narrative promises still other innovations in a literary career that shows no signs of slackening.

IV *The Mission of an Artist*

Using the exemplary novel of Cervantine inspiration as a means of carrying out a free and open scrutiny of human existence, Ayala probes with special intensity the issue of man's conduct and its motivations. His concern is fundamentally moral, but paradoxically he is not a moralist because he shares the weaknesses of his creatures, refusing to sermonize from a position of superiority. This is the implication of what occurs in *Dog's Death* when two narrator-protagonists, who are writers, become implicated in the very events they condemn. In man's weakness, however, lies his greatest strength, for Ayala's characters achieve the stature of veritable heroes when they come to grips with their conscience, though it be only for a brief moment in their harried lives. And lest readers should feel above these fallible creatures, the author's all-inclusive first-person plural implicates us all.

V *The Spanish Writer as World Mediator*

That the aspirations of this author, who so frequently employs plots, themes, and allusions from Spanish literature, go far beyond reaching a Hispanic public is evidenced in one of his key essays,

"Situación actual de la cultura española" ("The Present State of Spanish Culture"). Here Ayala perceives the existence of an identifiable cultural community based on characteristics traditionally assigned to both Latin Americans and Spaniards, namely individualism, personalism, and the law of *simpatía* (friendliness or personal inclination). While the Reformation with its emphasis on free thought, investigation, and enterprise provided the impetus for material progress in other Western countries, Spain has preserved, during the last four centuries, a somewhat archaic dedication to spiritual values, resisting the utilitarian impulse which brought the West to technical superiority. Unguided by spiritual values, technical progress has led to international rivalry and the possibility of nuclear destruction. Spanish culture, says Ayala, is in a unique position to offer a reorientation to a world which must find new ways to employ the vast power it now wields. The fact that Hispanic peoples are a cultural rather than political community can be used as an advantage since they do not represent a political threat. At the same time, recognizes Ayala, the lack of this type of hegemony makes it difficult for works written in Spanish to have international repercussions. This situation is lamentable because Hispanic literature, with its traditional dedication to individuality and problems of a moral nature, could help wind down the *ethos* of conquest inspired by technological advances and could thereby benefit individual cultures.[2]

Francisco Ayala's concern with this scrutiny of individual destiny and human values situates him in a long and respected line of Spanish authors, including Juan Ruiz, Fernando de Rojas, Miguel de Cervantes, Benito Pérez Galdós, and Miguel de Unamuno; but his attitude is perhaps even more heroic in our twentieth century when the Quixotic struggle is not against windmills of the Mancha but international monsters of technology which threaten man's freedom as an individual. Our author's prodigious artistic expression of preoccupation with these matters, therefore, is not only worthy of admiration in the Hispanic world, but of very special significance to world literature.

Notes and References

Chapter One

1. Rosario H. Hiriart, "Dos prólogos de Francisco Ayala," *Insula*, XXVII, 320 (January, 1972), 1.
2. Keith Ellis, *El arte narrativo de Francisco Ayala* (Madrid, 1964), pp. 12 - 13.
3. Francisco Ayala, *Confrontaciones* (Barcelona, 1972), p. 57.
4. *Ibid.*, p. 31.
5. See the first part of *Confrontaciones* which consists of nine such conversations between the author and different critics, and also the forthcoming book *Conversaciones con Francisco Ayala*, by Rosario H. Hiriart.

Chapter Two

1. Rosario H. Hiriart, *Las alusiones literarias en la obra narrativa de Francisco Ayala* (New York, 1972).
2. Francisco Ayala, *Obras narrativas completas* (Mexico, 1969), p. 598. All pages in parentheses in this chapter are from this edition, hereafter called *Complete Narrative Works*.
3. *Los ensayos: Teoría y crítica literaria* (Madrid, 1972), p. 1154.
4. Enrique Díez-Canedo, "Francisco Ayala: *Historia de un amanecer,*" *El Sol*, 15 (July 1926), p. 2; Ellis, p. 41; Andrés Amorós, Prologue to *Complete Narrative Works*, p. 26.
5. Ellis, p. 37.

Chapter Three

1. *Cazador en el alba y otras imaginaciones* (Barcelona, 1971), pp. 9 - 37.
2. Ayala, *Complete Narrative Works*, p. 598. All pages in parentheses in this chapter are from this edition.
3. "Lirismo en la prosa de Francisco Ayala," *Homenaje a Casalduero* (Madrid, 1972), pp. 141 - 150.

Chapter Four

1. "La invención del *Quijote,*" *Los ensayos* (Madrid, 1971), p. 639.
2. See "El arte de novelar y el oficio del novelista" in *Los ensayos*, pp. 541 - 554.

3. Soldevila Durante, "Vida en obra de Francisco Ayala," *La Torre* (Río Piedras, Puerto Rico), 42, (April - June 1963), 69 - 106, and Ellis, p. 61.

4. Miguel de Cervantes Saavedra, *El ingenioso hidalgo Don Quijote de la Mancha*, (Madrid, 1968), Part I: Cap. XL, p. 689.

5. All pages in parentheses in this chapter are from *Complete Narrative Works*.

6. Quoted in the prologue, p. 454, this comment originally appeared in *Sur*, XIV, 122 (December 1944), 58 - 59.

7. *Narrativa española fuera de España, 1939 - 1961* (Madrid, 1963), p. 247.

8. *Ibid.*, p. 248.

9. "El cuento 'El Inquisidor' de Francisco Ayala," in *Los usurpadores* (Barcelona, 1970), p. 214.

10. *Ibid.*, p. 221.

11. *Las alusiones literarias, p. 37.*

Chapter Five

1. All pages in parentheses in this chapter are from *Complete Narrative Works*.

2. In his prologue to *Ibid.*, p. 58.

3. "Responsabilidad y evasión en 'La cabeza del cordero,' " *Hispanófila* (September 1974), pp. 51 - 60.

4. This quotation is from Juan Ruiz, the Archpriest of Hita's *Libro de Buen Amor (Book of Good Love)*, written in 1330.

5. Hiriart, *Las alusiones literarias*, p. 69. The expression appears in the first act of *El alcalde de Zalamea*.

6. Ellis, p. 112.

Chapter Six

1. All pages in parentheses in this chapter are from *Complete Narrative Works*.

2. *Razón del mundo* (Xalapa, 1962), p. 52.

3. Ellis, p. 102.

4. *Las alusiones literarias*, pp. 59 - 60.

5. *El problema del liberalismo* (Río Piedras, 1963), pp. 28, 36, 180.

6. *Guy de Maupassant* (New York, 1973), p. 45.

7. Wallace, p. 44.

8. Wallace, p. 794.

9. Wallace, p. 792.

10. *Razón del mundo*, p. 82.

11. See "El escritor y su mundo," and especially the section "Para quién escribimos nosotros," in *Los ensayos*, pp. 138 - 164.

Chapter Seven

1. All pages in parentheses in this chapter are from *Complete Narrative Works*.
2. Francisco Ayala, *Mis páginas mejores* (Madrid, 1965), p. 20.
3. *Razón del mundo*, p. 90.
4. Ellis, p. 196.
5. "América en la narrativa de Francisco Ayala," *Cuadernos Hispanoamericanos*, 247 (July 1970), 269 - 72.
6. "La systematique des perspectives dans 'Muertes de perro,' " *Les Langues Neo-latines*, 187 (1968), 37 - 52.

Chapter Eight

1. All pages in this chapter are from *Complete Narrative Works*.
2. Rosario Hiriart points out abundant examples of military vocabulary in *Las alusiones literarias*, pp. 305 - 306.
3. "El punto de honor castellano," *Los ensayos*, p. 955.
4. Ayala has mentioned his newspaper source in conversation on several occasions.
5. Animal totems of this nature are described in Carl Jung, *Man and His Symbols* (New York, 1964).
6. *Mis páginas mejores* (Madrid, 1965), p. 277.
7. *Los ensayos*, p. 631.
8. *Ibid.*, p. 631.
9. Alberto Sánchez, "Cervantes y Francisco Ayala: original refundición de un cuento narrado en *El Quijote*," *Cauadernos Hispanoamericanos*, LXVI (1966), 133 - 139.
   Adrián García Montoro, "*El rapto*, novela ejemplar," *La Torre* (Río Piedras), XVI, 62 (October - December 1968), 151 - 165.
   Keith Ellis, "Cervantes and Ayala's *El rapto*: The Art of Reworking a Story," *Publications of the Modern Language Association*, LXXXIV, 1 (January 1969), 14 - 19.
10. Hiriart, *Las alusiones literarias*, pp. 203 - 259, and Estelle Irizarry, *Teoría y creación literaria en Francisco Ayala* (Madrid, 1971), 155 - 163, and in her edition of *El rapto*, (Barcelona, 1974), pp. 11 - 27.

Chapter Nine

1. *Confrontaciones*, pp. 133 - 147.
2. *Ibid.*, p. 146.
3. *Los ensayos: Teoría y crítica literaria*, pp. 333 - 346.
4. See Estelle Irizarry, *Teoría y creación literaria en Francisco Ayala*.
5. *Hoy ya es ayer* (Madrid, 1972).
6. *El problema del liberalismo* (Río Piedras, 1963). Selections are included in *Hoy ya es ayer* (see note 5), pp. 17 - 182.

7. *Razón del mundo.* Corresponds to *Hoy ya es ayer,* pp. 239 - 410.
8. *La crisis actual de la enseñanza* (Buenos Aires, 1958). Corresponds to "La crisis de la enseñanza" in *Hoy ya es ayer,* pp. 411 - 451.
9. *Tecnología y libertad* (Madrid, 1959). Corresponds to essays numbered 2 - 8 and 21 in *Los ensayos.*
10. *El escritor en la sociedad de masas* (Mexico, 1956 and Buenos Aires, 1958). Corresponds to essays numbered 1, 9 - 11, 15 and 20 in *Los ensayos.*
11. *De este mundo y el otro* (Barcelona, 1963). Corresponds to essays numbered 12 - 14 and 16 - 19 in *Los ensayos.*
12. *Complete Narrative Works,* p. 1147.

Chapter Ten

1. Andrés Amorós, "Conversación con Francisco Ayala," in *Confrontaciones,* p. 51.
2. *Los ensayos: Teoría y crítica literaria,* p. 682, hereafter called *Ensayos.*
3. All the studies mentioned in this chapter are found in *Ensayos.*
4. *Mis páginas mejores* (Madrid, 1965), pp. 7 - 20.
5. *Ensayos,* p. 1142.
6. *Ibid.,* p. 1155.
7. A complete list of these translations can be found in Andrés Amorós, *Bibliografía de Francisco Ayala* (Syracuse, 1973), pp. 75 - 76.
8. Published in 1970 by Taurus in Madrid and reproduced undated in *Ensayos,* pp. 387 - 430.
9. *Ensayos,* p. 393.
10. *Ibid.,* p. 395.

Chapter Eleven

1. Francisco Ayala, *El jardín de las delicias* (Barcelona, 1971), p. 16. All pages in parentheses in this chapter are from this edition.
2. *Las alusiones literarias,* p. 130.
3. It is obvious that the Spanish last name requires a euphemism for what it suggests, although Mier is a legitimate surname.
4. *La Nación* (Buenos Aires), 26 November 1972, Section 3, pp. 1 - 2.
5. *La Nación,* 8 July 1973, Section 3, p. 8.
6. Unpublished at this writing.
7. *Diálogos, Revista de El Colegio de México* (Guanajuato), 68 (March - April 1976), pp. 11 - 12.
8. Rosario Hiriart, "Metamorfosis de una anécdota: *Incidente* de Francisco Ayala (Un comentario de texto)," unpublished at the time of this writing.
9. In the article of the series entitled "Realidad imaginaria y realidad práctica," *La Nación,* 21 September 1975, Section 3, pp. 1 - 2.

10. Unpublished at this writing.
11. *La Nación*, 14 July 1974, Section 3 and *Diálogos, Revista de El Colegio de México* (Guanajuato), No. 58 (July - August 1974), p. 19.
12. Unpublished at this writing.
13. Unpublished at this writing.
14. Unpublished at this writing.
15. *Revista de Occidente* (Madrid), 129 (November 1973), pp. 159 - 168.
16. By a curious coincidence, the magazine *Espiral: Letras y Arte*, published in Bogotá, Colombia by the late Clemente Airó, published in its No. 132, in September 1974, a piece called "Vida sexual angélica" ("Angelic Sexual Life"), pp. 58 - 61. The author, Pedro Gómez Valderrama, refers to a debate on the subject which lasted five years in Constantinople in the late Middle Ages that only ended when the Turks invaded their meeting place. Gómez Valderrama suggests that a logical explanation for this perennial question of the angels' sexuality would be that there are two sexes, justifying the continuation of the species!

Chapter Twelve

1. Francisco Ayala, "Conversación sobre *El jardín de las delicias*," *Confrontaciones* (Barcelona, 1972), p. 102.
2. *Razón del mundo*, pp. 137 - 146. We have taken the risk of greatly simplifying what Ayala develops with careful and convincing arguments.

Selected Bibliography

The most comprehensive and definitive bibliography to date is Andrés Amorós's *Bibliografía de Francisco Ayala*, published by Syracuse University in 1973, containing 569 entries of primary and secondary materials.

PRIMARY SOURCES

Since Ayala's books alone are so numerous, we have omitted articles, book reviews, essays and other diverse material not yet incorporated into books.

1. Collections and Anthologies

Confrontaciones. Barcelona: Editorial Seix Barral, 1972. Includes interviews, Ayala's own prologues to his books, essays on writing, selected book reviews written by Ayala and fourteen photographs.

Cuentos. Salamanca, Madrid, Barcelona: Editorial Anaya, 1966. Second edition published as *El Inquisidor y otros cuentos.*

Los ensayos: Teoría y crítica literaria. Madrid: Aguilar, 1972. Prologue by Helio Carpintero. Essays.

El Hechizado y otros cuentos. Madrid: Magisterio Español, 1972. Introduction by José Luis Cano.

Hoy ya es ayer. Madrid: Editorial Moneda y Crédito, 1972. Essays.

Mis páginas mejores. Madrid: Editorial Gredos, 1965.

Obras narrativas completas. México: Aguilar, 1969. Complete narrative works of Ayala to 1969 in fourteen sections. Introduction by Andrés Amorós.

2. Books of Narrative

El as de Bastos. Buenos Aires: Sur, 1963.

El boxeador y un ángel. Madrid: Cuadernos Literarios, 1929.

La cabeza del cordero. Buenos Aires: Editorial Losada, 1949; Buenos Aires: Compañía General Fabril, 1962; Englewood Cliffs: Prentice Hall, 1968 (edited by Keith Ellis).

Cazador en el alba. Madrid: Ediciones Ulises, 1930; titled *Cazador en el alba y otras imaginaciones,* Barcelona: Seix Barral, 1971 (includes the stories of *El boxeador y un ángel* and prologue by José Carlos Mainer).

De raptos, violaciones y otras inconveniencias. Madrid-Barcelona: Alfaguara, 1966.

El fondo del vaso. Buenos Aires: Editorial Sudamericana, 1962; Madrid: Alianza Editorial, 1970.

157

El Hechizado. Buenos Aires: Cuadernos de la Quimera, Emecé, 1944.

Historia de macacos. Madrid: Revista de Occidente, 1955; Buenos Aires: Compañía Fabril Editora, 1964; Barcelona: Editorial Seix Barral, 1962.

Historia de un amanecer. Madrid: Editorial Castilla, 1926.

El jardín de las delicias. Barcelona: Editorial Seix Barral, 1971 and 1972. Premio de la Crítica.

Muertes de perro. Buenos Aires: Editorial Sudamericana, 1958; Madrid: Alianza Editorial, 1968.

El rapto. Madrid: La Novela Popular, 1965; *El rapto, Student Edition*, New York: Harcourt, Brace, Jovanovich, 197 (edited by Phyllis Zatlin Boring, for intermediate reading courses). *El rapto, Fragancia de jazmines, Diálogo entre el amor y un viejo*, Barcelona: Editorial Labor, 1974 (edition and introduction by Estelle Irizarry).

Tragicomedia de un hombre sin espíritu. Madrid: Industrial Gráfica, 1925.

Los usurpadores. Buenos Aires: Editorial Sudamericana, 1949; Barcelona: Editorial Andorra, 1970; Barcelona: Editorial Seix Barral, 1971.

3.   In English Translation

"The Bewitched" ("El Hechizado") in *Spanish Writers in Exile*, Sansolito: Bern Porter, 1950 (editor Angel Flores).

Death as a Way of Life. New York: Macmillan; London: Michael Joseph, 1965, translated by Joan MacLean. Because of the limited availability of the English translation and the preference of the author of the novel, we refer to it in our text with the title *Dog's Death*.

4.   Books of Essays

Breve teoría de la traducción. México: Obregón, 1956. As *Problemas de la traducción*, Madrid: Taurus, 1965.

La crisis actual de la enseñanza. Buenos Aires: Editorial Nova, 1958.

De este mundo y el otro. Barcelona: E.D.H.A.S.A., 1963.

El derecho social en la constitución de la República española. Madrid: M. Minuesa de los Ríos, 1932.

Derechos de la persona individual para una sociedad de masas. Buenos Aires: Perrot, 1953.

Una doble experiencia política: España e Italia (Coauthor: Renato Treves). México: El Colegio de México, 1944.

Ensayo sobre la libertad. México: Fondo de Cultura Económica, 1945.

Ensayos de sociología política. México: Instituto de Investigaciones Sociales, 1952.

El escritor en la sociedad de masas. México: Obregón, 1956; Buenos Aires: Sur, 1958.

El escritor y su imagen (Ortega y Gasset, Azorín, Valle-Inclán, Antonio Machado). Madrid: Ediciones Guadarrama, 1975.

España, a la fecha. Buenos Aires: Sur, 1965.

La evasión de los intelectuales (Coauthor: H. A. Murena). México: Centro de Estudios y Documentación Sociales.

Los políticos. Buenos Aires: Editorial Depalma, 1944.

El problema del liberalismo. México: Fondo de Cultura Económica, 1941; revised edition Río Piedras, Puerto Rico: University of Puerto Rico, 1963.

Razón del mundo. Buenos Aires: Editorial Losada, 1944; revised edition Xalapa: Universidad Veracruzana, 1962.

Realidad y ensueño. Madrid: Editorial Gredos, 1963.

Reflexiones sobre la estructura narrativa. Madrid: Taurus, 1970.

Tecnología y libertad. Madrid: Taurus, 1959.

Tratado de sociología. Buenos Aires: Editorial Losada, 1947; Madrid: Aguilar, 1961, 1968.

Experiencia e invención. Madrid: Taurus, 1960.

Historia de la libertad. Buenos Aires: Atlántida, 1942.

Histrionismo y representación. Buenos Aires: Editorial Sudamericana, 1944.

Indagación del cinema. Madrid: Mundo Latino, 1929. Enlarged edition as *El cine, arte y espectáculo,* Buenos Aires: Argos, 1949 and revised and enlarged Xalapa: Universidad Veracruzana, 1966.

La integración social en América. Buenos Aires: Editorial Nova, 1958.

Introducción a las ciencias sociales. Madrid: Aguilar, 1952.

La invención del "Quijote." Río Piedras, Puerto Rico: Editorial Universitaria, 1950.

Jovellanos. Buenos Aires: Centro Asturiano, 1945.

El "Lazarillo" reexaminado. Nuevo examen de algunos aspectos. Madrid: Taurus, 1971.

Oppenheimer. México: Fondo de Cultura Económica, 1942.

El pensamiento vivo de Saavedra Fajardo. Buenos Aires: Editorial Losada, 1941.

SECONDARY SOURCES

1. Books

ELLIS, KEITH. *El arte narrativo de Francisco Ayala.* Madrid: Editorial Gredos, 1964. First book devoted completely to Ayala. Concentrates on his narrative techniques up to and including *The Bottom of the Glass.* Limited largely to stylistic considerations, with good biography and bibliography.

HIRIART, ROSARIO H. *Las alusiones literarias en la obra narrativa de Francisco Ayala.* New York: Eliseo Torres and Sons, 1972. Excellent guidebook to the use and identification of many literary allusions. One chapter covers most of Ayala's works briefly, while chapters are individually dedicated to "Dialogues of Love," Fragrance of Jas-

mines," *The Abduction* and "A Resounding Wedding." Very compe-
tent treatment of a difficult subject.

————. *Los recursos técnicos en la novelística de Francisco Ayala.*
Madrid: Insula, 1972. Contains six diverse studies with very selected
examples on the theme of time, use of musical compositions, names,
universal aspects of *Dog's Death* and *The Bottom of the Glass* and
the basic theme of man in his world.

IRIZARRY, ESTELLE. *Teoría y creación literaria en Francisco Ayala.*
Madrid: Editorial Gredos, 1971. Relates Ayala's discursive works to
illuminate and interpret his fictions, with regard to motivation,
themes, "negative" materials, humor, perspective, novelty of plot
and prose style. Examines how Ayala applies his own criteria in
writing fiction.

2.   Chapters and Sections in Longer Works

AMORÓS, ANDRÉS. "Prólogo," *Obras narrativas completas.* México, D. F.:
Aguilar, 1969. A brief but excellent review of the narrative works included, with a number of good insights.

————. "Prólogo," *Los usurpadores.* Barcelona: Editorial Andorra, 1970.
Contains rather general comments on the stories of the volume.

CARPINTERO, HELIO. "Francisco Ayala, intelectual en dos mundos," *Cinco
aventuras españolas.* Madrid: Editorial Revista de Occidente, 1967,
pp. 25 - 62. A general discussion of Ayala's ideas, particularly with
regard to Spain, as revealed in his essays. Points out their importance
in his imaginative creations but stops short of illustrating this point.

————. "Prólogo," to Ayala's *Los ensayos: Teoría y crítica literaria.*
Madrid: Aguilar, 1972, pp. xi - xxxi. Considers Ayala's motives in
writing essays and his importance in Spanish letters. Contains brief
references to specific books of essays, with discussion of some social,
historical and ideological elements.

ELLIS, KEITH. "El enfoque literario de la Guerra Civil española: Malraux
y Ayala," preceding the fictions of Ayala's *La cabeza del cordero.*
Buenos Aires: Compañía General Fabril Editora, 1962, pp. 9 - 23.
Comparative study of Malraux's "L'Espoir" and Ayala's "El Tajo,"
which finds the latter superior aesthetically.

IRIZARRY, ESTELLE. Introduction to edition of *El rapto, Fragancia de jazmines, Diálogo entre el amor y un viejo.* Barcelona: Editorial Labor,
1974. pp. 7 - 36. Analytical and interpretative study of each of the
works included in the edition with copious notes.

MAINER, JOSÉ CARLOS. "Perfil de un escritor contemporáneo," introduction to Ayala's *Cazador en el alba y otras imaginaciones.* Barcelona:
Editorial Seix Barral, 1971, pp. 9 - 37. Situates Ayala's vanguard fictions in the literature of the twenties and thirties. Contains a very
useful discussion of four vanguard characteristics: the "new" psychology, metaphorical vision, cosmopolitanism and humor.

MARRA-LÓPEZ, JOSÉ R. *Narrativa española fuera de España (1939 - 1961).*
Madrid: Ediciones Guadarrama, 1963. "Francisco Ayala. Una con-

ciencia lúcida," pp. 217 - 282. A general survey of the evolution of Ayala's work up to and including *Dog's Death*. Important for bringing the author before the Spanish reading public. Informational with significant insights.

MOLINA, RODRIGO A. *Estudios*. Madrid: Insula, 1961. "*Muertes de perro: Triple dimensión*," pp. 9 - 32. Despite a rather debatable emphasis on original sin and its consequences, contains a discussion of Calderonian techniques and treats vocabulary, idioms and style in *Dog's Death*.

NORA, EUGENIO G. DE. *La novela española contemporánea (1927 - 1960)*, III. Madrid: Editorial Gredos, 1968, pp. 243 - 255. Schematic review of Ayala's narrative up to and including *The Bottom of the Glass*. Tends to over-emphasize sociological and moralistic interpretation, but is important in establishing Ayala firmly as a literary artist.

RODRÍGUEZX-ALCALÁ, HUGO. *Ensayos de Norte a Sur*. Seattle: University of Washington Press and México, D.F.: Ediciones de Andrea, 1960, pp. 61 - 80. Contains two studies, primarily on *Dog's Death*, and a brief note on *Monkey Story*. Distinguishes three stages in Ayala's fictions: early metaphorical style, followed by emotional compassion for his creatures and finally, cruel, annihilating satire. This last view has been echoed by a number of critics, but has been refuted by Ayala and other critics.

3. Major Articles in Periodicals and Related Publications (A few representative articles on particularly interesting themes, with emphasis on more recent studies which take into account a major portion of Ayala's work. Reviews of specific works are excluded because they are so numerous.)

BLANCO AMOR, JOSÉ. "América en la narrativa de Francisco Ayala," *Cuadernos Hispanoamericanos*, 247 (July 1970), 269 - 72. Brief but valuable consideration of the influence of the Americas in Ayala's work.

ELLIS, KEITH. "Cervantes and Ayala's *El rapto*: The Art of Reworking a Story," *PMLA*, LXXXIV, no. 1 (January 1969), 14 - 19. The only major article on Ayala in English, except for reviews. Examines meaning and structure involved in *The Abduction*, interpreting its similarities to Cervantes's story as a demonstration of the "tendency of human weaknesses to repeat themselves." Should be read in connection with other materials on the subject.

GIL, ILDEFONSO-MANUEL. "Lirismo en la prosa de Francisco Ayala," *Homenaje a Casalduero*. Madrid: Editorial Gredos, 1972. pp. 141 - 50. A very perceptive essay analyzing Ayala's intensified lyricism in narrative after 1969 as one perspective of an author capable of complementing and contrasting different modes of expression without sacrificing his internal unity.

INSULA, Año XXVII, no. 302 (January 1972). An issue concentrating on Ayala, with the following articles and other materials: Andrés Amorós: "Conversación con Francisco Ayala sobre 'El jardín de las delicias,' " reproducing an interview. José Luis Cano: "Francisco Ayala." General tribute to the author. Rosario H. Hiriart: "Dos prólogos de Francisco Ayala." Discusses the prologues of *The Usurpers* and *The Abduction*. Estelle Irizarry: "Lo divino, lo profano y el arte en nuevos 'Días felices' de Francisco Ayala." Studies connotations of sacred and profane allusions and explains the function of art works in "Happy Days." Antonio Martínez Herrarte: " 'Historia de macacos' o el descenso a los infiernos." Sees irony turned satire in *"Monkey Story."*

JOLY, MONIQUE. "La systématique des perspectives dans 'Muertes de perro'," *Les Langues Néo-Latines*, 63 année, no. 187 (1968), 37 - 52. A fine analysis of Ayala's handling of perspective, language, names, narrative person, reappearances, and contrasting versions to enhance reality in *Dog's Death*.

ORRINGER, NELSON. "Responsabilidad y evasión en 'La cabeza del cordero,' " *Hispanófila* (September 1974), pp. 51 - 60. In-depth study of the theme of responsibility and evasion with concrete illustrations in *The Lamb's Head*.

SOLDEVILA DURANTE, IGNACIO. "Vida en obra de Francisco Ayala," *La Torre* (Río Piedras, Puerto Rico), 42 (April - June 1963), pp. 69 - 106. An important early article which points out unifying elements in Ayala's production with references to fictions, essays and prologues.

Index

(The works of Ayala are listed under his name)

163